Revolution and Romanticism, 1789-1834
A series of facsimile reprints chosen and introduced by
Jonathan Wordsworth
University Lecturer in Romantic Studies at Oxford

Shelley
The Cenci 1819

Percy Bysshe Shelley

The Cenci
1819

Woodstock Books
Oxford and New York
1991

This edition first published 1991 by
Woodstock Books
Spelsbury House, Spelsbury, Oxford OX7 3JR
and
Woodstock Books
Wordsworth Trust America
Department of English, City College
Convent Ave and 138th St, New York, N.Y. 10031

New matter copyright © Woodstock Books 1991
Reproduced by permission from a copy in the
Bodleian Library, Oxford, Shelfmark Don d.130

British Library Cataloguing in Publication Data
Shelley, Percy Bysshe, 1792-1822
    The Cenci 1819. – (Revolution and romanticism,
    1789-1834)
    I. Title   II. Series
    822.7
    ISBN 1-85477-078-0

Printed and bound in Great Britain by
Smith Settle
Otley, West Yorkshire LS21 3JP

Introduction

Tragedies are rare. Many plays, poems, novels, have unhappy endings, but tragic intensity is achieved by few writers, and only in a small proportion of their works. Implied is an intuition into the very nature of suffering. The reader (audience) must identify with pain, yet finally stand outside it. There must be the overwhelming sense of waste identified long ago by A. C. Bradley (*Oxford Lectures on Shakespeare*, 1904), together with admiration and an enhancing sense of human dignity. We must be made to feel both the littleness of man, defeated and transient, and outrage that anything so great should be caused to suffer, permitted to die. We must endure with Lear as he bends in the final scene over the body of Cordelia:

> No, no, no life!
> Why should a dog, a horse, a rat, have life,
> And thou no breath at all? Thou'lt come no more,
> Never, never, never, never, never.
> Pray you undo this button. Thank you, sir.
> Do you see this? Look on her! Look her lips,
> Look there, look there!
>
> > [*He dies*]

That Shelley should have such power comes as a surprise. His poetry is full of passion, but does not commonly deal in the sharpness of pain. That he should have written *The Cenci* between Acts Three and Four of *Prometheus unbound* seems more surprising still. The grandeur of *Prometheus*, outside time, unlimited in space, contracts to the history of a single fated household in late renaissance Rome. It is Cenci himself who forms the link. Even the knowledge that he did exist, that there was once such a human being, does not make credible the horror of his actions. He has about him the axiomatic malignity of Jove. We could, if we chose, regard him as a sadist, a psychopath, but we don't – tragedy does not deal in diagnoses – we see him as a force, a prodigious manifestation of hatred. Monstrous as they are, his actions seem less evil than those of the Pope, who condones his murders in return for gold, or of Orsino, who connives and prompts in order to entrap Beatrice for himself. Evil in *The Cenci* consists in hypocrisy and self-serving. The Count stoops to neither.

The question as to what goodness consists of is more difficult. Apart from Cardinal Camillo, who is well-intentioned despite excessive wealth, and Bernardo Cenci (the pardoned younger brother), those with whom we sympathize are murderers. Beatrice, hero of the tragedy, is unhesitating in the decision to kill her father, and never for a moment repents. Whether she is more sinned against than sinning, depends on how one weighs brutality, rape and incest, on the one hand, against parricide on the other. Either way, the innocence in which she entirely believes is of an unusual kind. Of Shelley's numerous reviewers, all but two were profoundly shocked. It is the Reverend George Croly who sets the tone in the *Literary gazette* of 1 April 1820:

Of all the abominations which intellectual perverseness, and poetical atheism, have produced in our times, this tragedy appears to us the most abominable.

According to the *Edinburgh monthly review*, in May, Shelley has been tempted to 'withdraw the veil from things that ought for ever to remain concealed'.

Even John Scott, in Baldwin's *London magazine* (also May 1820), turns from his praise of sublimity and tenderness in the poetry to consider Shelley's depravity and 'weakness of character'. 'This extraordinary work', he writes,

preserves throughout a vigorous, clear, manly turn of expression, of which [Shelley] makes excellent use to give force, and even sublimity, to the flashes of passion and of phrenzy – and wildness and horror to the darkness of cruelty and guilt. His language, as he travels through the most exaggerated incidents, retains its correctness and simplicity . . .

There are 'the most beautiful images, the most delicate and finished ornaments of sentiment and description'.

There is 'the most touching tenderness, graceful sorrow, and solemn appalling misery' that constitutes 'the very genius of poesy',

but, strange and lamentable to say, closely connected with [these are] the signs of a depraved, nay mawkish, or rather emasculated, moral taste, craving after trash, filth and poison . . .

Nothing in the play supports this judgment. Lurid details are excluded. There are no erotic or violent scenes. Cenci's abuse of Beatrice takes place off stage, and is never described. Shelley does not so much as mention the word, incest.

Like Byron's *Cain*, in the following year, *The Cenci* is morally offensive to the age in which it is written. Its subject is taboo. Shelley's own view of his material is set out in the Preface, a document of considerable importance in its own right. Far from showing a depraved pleasure in the horrors, he is anxious that they should be treated in a way that plays down their sensationalism. His interest has been aroused by Guido's portrait of Beatrice at the Colonna Palace. He has obtained the copy of a manuscript describing her story, and wishes to tell it, 'endeavouring as nearly as possible to represent the characters as they probably were':

This story of the Cenci is indeed eminently fearful and monstrous: any thing like a dry exhibition of it on the stage would be insupportable. The person who would treat such a subject must increase the ideal, and diminish the actual horror of the events, so that the pleasure which arises from the poetry that exists in these tempestuous sufferings and crimes may mitigate the pain of the contemplation of the moral deformity from which they spring.

The concept of poetry as innate within the 'tempestuous sufferings and crimes' of the past seemed meaningless to at least one of the reviewers, but follows from Shelley's wish to be true – imaginatively true – to the emotion he portrays. 'The Reader cannot be too often reminded', Wordsworth had written in his Note to *The thorn* (1800), 'that Poetry is passion: it is the history or science of feelings'.

Like Wordsworth, Shelley refuses to inculcate a moral. Purpose is innate in his writing, just as poetry is innate in the feelings that he hopes to recreate:

There must . . . be nothing attempted to make the exhibition subservient to what is vulgarly termed a moral purpose. The highest moral purpose aimed at in the highest species of the drama, is the teaching the human heart, through its sympathies and antipathies, the knowledge of itself; in proportion to the possession of which knowledge, every human being is wise, just, sincere, tolerant and kind.

In what might seem a mood of unusual tolerance, Shelley adds, 'If dogmas can do more, it is well: but a drama is no fit place for the enforcement of them.' His characters are 'represented as Catholics', and as such, 'deeply tinged with religion.' Their religion, however, has no bearing on moral conduct, and none on how the play is to be perceived. Catholicism in Italy

pervades intensely the whole frame of society, and is according to the temper of the mind which it inhabits, a passion, a persuasion, an excuse, a refuge; never a check.

Cenci, Shelley records, 'built a chapel in the court of his Palace', dedicated to St Thomas the Apostle, 'and established masses for the peace of his soul'.

Beatrice, her brother and step-mother, were not right to kill Cenci; but nor, in the terms of the tragedy, were they wrong. He was violent, cruel, a murderer many times over. They took the law into their own hands. Giacomo and Lucretia confess at once under torture: Beatrice does not. In her own eyes she is innocent. It is in this larger moral vision that the greatness of the tragedy lies. Beatrice kills her father, as Tess kills Alec D'Urberville, to put right an intolerable wrong. Neither could have behaved otherwise. Hardy goes so far as to subtitle his book, *A pure woman*; Shelley is not (on this occasion) out to shock his critics. He merely gives to Beatrice the tragic stature, and tragic climax, that his contemporaries felt to have been forfeited. 'One thing more, my child', she says to the young Bernardo, in the final scene

> For thine own sake be constant to the love
> Thou bearest us; and to the faith that I,
> Tho' wrapt in a strange cloud of crime and shame,
> Lived ever holy and unstained . . .

Bernardo]   I cannot say, farewell!

Camillo]   O, Lady Beatrice!

Beatrice]   Give yourself no unnecessary pain,
My dear Lord Cardinal. Here, Mother, tie
My girdle for me, and bind up this hair
In any simple knot; aye, that does well.
And yours I see is coming down. How often
Have we done this for one another; now
We shall not do it any more. My Lord,
We are quite ready. Well, 'tis very well.

In the background we hear Lear's 'Pray you undo this button', but it is not an imitation, or a borrowing, it is a beautiful acknowledgement from one great tragic writer to another. Hunt, in the *Indicator* for 26 July 1820, comments that Shelley

reminds us of some of the most strenuous and daring of our old dramatists, not by any means as an imitator, though he has studied them, but as a bold, elemental imagination, and a framer of 'mighty lines'.

To which he adds, conscious no doubt of the affront that it will give,

He possesses also . . . what those to whom we more particularly allude did not possess, great sweetness of nature, and enthusiasm for good; and his style is, as it ought to be, the offspring of this high mixture.

Hunt is thinking of Marlowe ('framer of *mighty lines*', and Tourneur, and Middleton's *Changeling* (with its very different Beatrice, also wrapped in a 'cloud of crime and shame'); but Shelley's 'great sweetness of nature, and enthusiasm for good' could well be said to distinguish him from Shakespeare too. *The Cenci*'s 'high mixture' of style is carefully devised. Shelley has, he tells us, avoided 'the introduction of what is commonly called mere poetry': 'In a dramatic composition the imagery and the passion should interpenetrate one another, the former being reserved simply for the full developement and illustration of the latter.' Inevitably there are the too Shakespearean moments, but Shelley, like the Byron of *Cain* and *Sardanapalus*, has created a vivid unmetaphorical blank verse that is all his own.

To the strangely open-minded reviewer of the *Theatrical inquisitor* (April 1820) it seemed that there was a 'dark splendor' to Shelley's genius:

As a first dramatic effort, *The Cenci* is unparalleled for the beauty of every attribute with which the drama can be endowed. It has few errors but such as time will amend, and many beauties that time can neither strengthen nor abate.

Hunt thought the play 'undoubtedly the greatest dramatic production of the day' (*Examiner*, 19 March 1820), but was of course writing the year before Byron's *Three plays* appeared. Mary Shelley commented interestingly, and perhaps rightly, that Act V of *The Cenci* is the greatest thing that Shelley ever wrote. The final speech of Beatrice establishes him among the few great English tragic writers.

J W

THE CENCI.

A TRAGEDY,

IN FIVE ACTS.

By PERCY B. SHELLEY.

———⊷⊶———

ITALY.

PRINTED FOR C. AND J. OLLIER
VERE STREET, BOND STREET.
LONDON.
1819.

DEDICATION

T O
LEIGH HUNT ESQ.

———◦————

MY DEAR FRIEND,

I inscribe with your name, from a distant country, and after an absence whose months have seemed years, this the latest of my literary efforts.

Those writings which I have hitherto published, have been little else than visions which impersonate my own appre-

hensions of the beautiful and the just.
I can also perceive in them the literary defects incidental to youth and im-
patience; they are dreams of what ought
to be, or may be. The drama which I
now present to you is a sad reality. I lay
aside the presumptuous attitude of an
instructor, and am content to paint,
with such colours as my own heart fur-
nishes, that which has been.

Had I known a person more highly
endowed than yourself with all that it
becomes a man to possess, I had soli-
cited for this work the ornament of his
name. One more gentle, honourable,
innocent and brave; one of more exalt-
ed toleration for all who do and think
evil, and yet himself more free from evil;
one who knows better how to receive,
and how to confer a benefit though he
must ever confer far more than he can
receive; one of simpler, and, in the
highest sense of the word, of purer
life and manners I never knew: and I
had already been fortunate in friend-

ships when your name was added to the list .

In that patient and irreconcileable enmity with domestic and political tyranny and imposture which the tenor of your life has illustrated, and which, had I health and talents should illustrate mine, let us, comforting each other in our task, live and die.

All happiness attend you!

Your affectionate friend,
PERCY B. SHELLEY.

Rome, May 29. 1819.

PREFACE

A Manuscript was communicated to me during my travels in Italy which was copied from the archives of the Cenci Palace at Rome, and contains a detailed account of the horrors which ended in the extinction of one of the noblest and richest families of that city during the Pontificate of Clement VIII, in the year, 1599. The story is, that an old man having spent his life in debauchery and wickedness, conceived at length an implacable hatred towards his children; which shewed itself towards one daughter under the form of an incestuous passion, aggravated by every circumstance of cruelty and violence. This daughter, after long and vain attempts to escape from what she considered a perpetual contamination both of body and mind, at length plotted with her mother-in-law and brother to murder their common tyrant. The young maiden who was urged to this tremendous deed by an impulse which overpowered its horror, was evidently a most gentle and amiable being, a creature formed to adorn and be admired, and thus violently thwarted from her nature by the necessity of circumstance and opinion. The deed was quickly discovered and in spite of the most earnest prayers made to the Pope by the highest persons in Rome the criminals were put to death. The old man had during his life repeatedly bought his pardon from the Pope for capital crimes of the most enormous and unspeakable kind, at the price of a hundred thousand crowns; the death therefore of his victims can scarcely be accounted for by the love of justice. The Pope, among other motives for severity, pro-

bably felt that whoever killed the Count Cenci deprived his
treasury of a certain and copious source of revenue. The
Papal Government formerly took the most extraordinary
precautions against the publicity of facts which offer so
tragical a demonstration of its own wickedness and weakness; so that the communication of the M. S. had become,
until very lately, a matter of some difficulty. Such a story, if told so as to present to the reader all the feelings of
those who once acted it, their hopes and fears, their confi-
dences and misgivings, their various interests, passions and
opinions acting upon and with each other, yet all conspiring to one tremendous end, would be as a light to make
apparent some of the most dark and secret caverns of the
human heart.

On my arrival at Rome I found that the story of the
Cenci was a subject not to be mentioned in Italian society
without awakening a deep and breathless interest; and
that the feelings of the company never failed to incline to
a romantic pity for the wrongs, and a passionate exculpa-
tion of the horrible deed to which they urged her, who
has been mingled two centuries with the common dust. All
ranks of people knew the outlines of this history, and parti-
cipated in the overwhelming interest which it seems to
have the magic of exciting in the human heart. I had a
copy of Guido's picture of Beatrice which is preserved in
the Colonna Palace, and my servant instantly recognized it
as the portrait of *La Cenci.*

This national and universal interest which the story
produces and has produced for two centuries and among
all ranks of people in a great City, where the imagination is
kept for ever active and awake, first suggested to me the

conception of its fitness for a dramatic purpose. In fact it
is a tragedy which has already received from its capacity
of awakening and sustaining the sympathy of men, appro-
bation and success. Nothing remained as I imagined, but
to clothe it to the apprehensions of my countrymen in such
language and action as would bring it home to their hearts·
The deepest and the sublimest tragic compositions, King
Lear and the two plays in which the tale of Ædipus is
told, were stories which already existed in tradition, as
matters of popular belief and interest, before Shakspeare
and Sophocles made them familiar to the sympathy of all
succeeding generations of mankind.

This story of the Cenci is indeed eminently fearful and
monstrous: any thing like a dry exhibition of it on the
stage would be insupportable. The person who would treat
such a subject must increase the ideal, and diminish the
actual horror of the events, so that the pleasure which
arises from the poetry which exists in these tempestuous
sufferings and crimes may mitigate the pain of the contemplation of the moral deformity from which they spring.
There must also be nothing attempted to make the exhibition subservient to what is vulgarly termed a moral purpose. The highest moral purpose aimed at in the highest
species of the drama, is the teaching the human heart,
through its sympathies and antipathies, the knowledge of
itself; in proportion to the possession of which knowledge,
every human being is wise, just, sincere, tolerant and kind.
If dogmas can do more, it is well: but a drama is no fit
place for the enforcement of them. Undoubtedly, no person can be truly dishonoured by the act of another; and
the fit return to make to the most enormous injuries is

kindness and forbearance, and a resolution to convert the
injurer from his dark passions by peace and love. Revenge,
retaliation, atonement, are pernicious mistakes. If Beatrice
had thought in this manner she would have been wiser and
better; but she would never have been a tragic character:
the few whom such an exhibition would have interested,
could never have been sufficiently interested for a dramatic
purpose, from the want of finding sympathy in their interest among the mass who surround them. It is in the restless
and anatomizing casuistry with which men seek the justification of Beatrice, yet feel that she has done what needs justification; it is in the superstitious horror with which they
contemplate alike her wrongs and their revenge; that the
dramatic character of what she did and suffered, consists.

I have endeavoured as nearly as possible to represent the
characters as they probably were, and have sought to avoid
the error of making them actuated by my own conceptions
of right or wrong, false or true thus under a thin veil
converting names and actions of the sixteenth century into
cold impersonations of my own mind. They are represented
as Catholics, and as Catholics deeply tinged with religion.
To a Protestant apprehension there will appear something
unnatural in the earnest and perpetual sentiment of the
relations between God and man which pervade the tragedy of the Cenci. It will especially be startled at the
combination of an undoubting persuasion of the truth of
the popular religion with a cool and determined perseverance in enormous guilt. But religion in Italy is not, as in
protestant countries, a cloak to be worn on particular days;
or a passport which those who do not wish to be railed at
carry with them to exhibit; or a gloomy passion for pene-

trating the impenetrable mysteries of our being, which terrifies its possessor at the darkness of the abyss to the brink of which it has conducted him. Religion coexists, as it were, in the mind of an Italian Catholic with a faith in that of which all men have the most certain knowledge. It is interwoven with the whole fabric of life. It is adoration, faith, submission, penitence, blind admiration; not a rule for moral conduct. It has no necessary connexion with any one virtue. The most atrocious villain may be rigidly devout, and without any shock to established faith, confess himself to be so. Religion pervades intensely the whole frame of society, and is according to the temper of the mind which it inhabits, a passion, a persuasion, an excuse, a refuge; never a check. Cenci himself built a chapel in the court of his Palace, and dedicated it to St. Thomas the Apostle, and established masses for the peace of his soul. Thus in the first scene of the fourth act Lucretia's design in exposing herself to the consequences of an expostulation with Cenci after having administered the opiate, was to induce him by a feigned tale to confess himself before death; this being esteemed by Catholics as essential to salvation; and she only relinquishes her purpose when she perceives that her perseverance would expose Beatrice to new outrages.

I have avoided with great care in writing this play the introduction of what is commonly called mere poetry, and I imagine there will scarcely be found a detached simile or a single isolated description, unless Beatrice's description of the chasm appointed for her father's murder should be judged to be of that nature (*).

(*) An idea in this speech was suggested by a most sublime passage

In a dramatic composition the imagery and the passion should interpenetrate one another, the former being reserved simply for the full developement and illustration of the latter. Imagination is as the immortal God which should assume flesh for the redemption of mortal passion. It is thus that the most remote and the most familiar imagery may alike be fit for dramatic purposes when employed in the illustration of strong feeling, which raises what is low, and levels to the apprehension that which is lofty, casting over all the shadow of its own greatness. In other respects I have written more carelessly; that is, without an over-fastidious and learned choice of words. In this respect I entirely agree with those modern critics who assert that in order to move men to true sympathy we must use the familiar language of men. And that our great ancestors the antient English poets are the writers, a study of whom might incite us to do that for our own age which they have done for theirs. But it must be the real language of men in general and not that of any particular class to whose society the writer happens to belong. So much for what I have attempted; I need not be assured that success is a very different matter; particularly for one whose attention has but newly been awakened to the study of dramatic literature.

I endeavoured whilst at Rome to observe such monuments of this story as might be accessible to a stranger The portrait of Beatrice at the Colonna Palace is most admirable as a work of art: it was taken by Guido dur-

in « El Purgatorio de San Patricio » of Calderon: the only plagiarism which I have intentionally committed in the whole piece.

ing her confinement in prison . But it is most interesting as a just representation of one of the loveliest specimens of the workmanship of Nature . There is a fixed and pale composure upon the features : she seems sad and stricken down in spirit, yet the despair thus expressed is lightened by the patience of gentleness . Her head is bound with folds of white drapery from which the yellow strings of her golden hair escape, and fall about her neck. The moulding of her face is exquisitely delicate; the eye brows are distinct and arched: the lips have that permanent meaning of imagination and sensibility which suffering has not repressed and which it seems as if death scarcely could extinguish . Her forehead is large and clear; her eyes which we are told were remarkable for their vivacity, are swollen with weeping and lustreless , but beautifully tender and serene. In the whole mien there is a simplicity and dignity which united with her exquisite loveliness and deep sorrow are inexpressib'y pathetic . Beatrice Cenci appears to have been one of those rare persons in whom energy and gentleness dwell together without destroying one another : her nature was simple and profound. The crimes and miseries in which she was an actor and a sufferer are as the mask and the mantle in which circumstances clothed her for her impersonation on the scene of the world.

The Cenci Palace is of great extent ; and though in part modernized , there yet remains a vast and gloomy pile of feudal architecture in the same state as during the dreadful scenes which are the subject of this tragedy. The Palace is situated in an obscure corner of·Rome , near the quarter of the Jews , and from the upper windows you see the immense ruins of Mount Palatine half hidden under their profuse overgrowth of trees. There is a court in one part of the palace (perhaps that in which Cenci built the Chapel to St. Thomas), supported by granite columns and adorned with antique friezes of fine workmanship and built up, according to the antient Italian fashion, with balcony over balcony of open work . One of the gates of the palace formed of immense stones and leading through a passage, dark and lofty and opening into gloomy subterranean chambers, struck me particularly .

Of the Castle of Petrella , I could obtain no further information than that which is to be found in the manuscript.

THE CENCI.

DRAMATIS PERSONAE.

COUNT FRANCESCO CENCI.

GIACOMO.
BERNARDO. } his sons.

CARDINAL CAMILLO.

ORSINO, A PRELATE.

SAVELLA, the Pope's Legate.

OLIMPIO.
MARZIO. } Assassins.

ANDREA, servant to Cenci.

Nobles - Judges - Guards - Servants.

LUCRETIA, Wife of Cenci, and step-mother of his children.

BEATRICE, his daughter.

The Scene lies principally in Rome, but changes during the fourth Act to Petrella a castle among the Apulia Apennines.
Time. During the Pontificate of Clement VIII.

THE CENCI

ACT I.

SCENE I.

An apartment in the CENCI *Palace.*
Enter COUNT CENCI, *and* CARDINAL CAMILLO

Cam. That matter of the murder is hushed up
If you consent to yield his Holiness
Your fief that lies beyond the Pincian gate. –
It needed all my interest in the conclave
To bend him to this point: he said that you
Bought perilous impunity with your gold;
That crimes like yours if once or twice compounded
Enriched the Church, and respited from hell
An erring soul which might repent and live: –
But that the glory and the interest
Of the high throne he fills, little consist
With making it a daily mart of guilt
So manifold and hideous as the deeds
Which you scarce hide from men's revolted eyes.
Cen. The third of my possessions – let it go!
Aye, I once heard the nephew of the Pope
Had sent his architect to view the ground,

Meaning to build a villa on my vines
The next time I compounded with his uncle:
I little thought he should outwit me so!
Henceforth no witness - not the lamp - shall see
That which the vassal threatened to divulge
Whose throat is choked with dust for his reward.
The deed he saw could not have rated higher
That his most worthless life: - it angers me!
Respited from Hell! - So may the Devil
Respite their souls from Heaven. No doubt Pope
   Clement,
And his most charitable nephews, pray
That the apostle Peter and the saints
Will grant for their sake that I long enjoy
Strength, wealth, and pride, and lust, and length
   of days
Wherein to act the deeds which are the stewards
Of their revenue. - But much yet remains
To which they shew no title.
 Cam.   Oh, Count Cenci!
So much that thou migh'st honourably live
And reconcile thyself with thine own heart
And with thy God, and with the offended world.
How hideously look deeds of lust and blood
Thro' those snow white and venerable hairs! -
Your children should be sitting round you now,
But that you fear to read upon their looks
The shame and misery you have written there.
Where is your wife? Where is your gentle
   daughter?

Methinks her sweet looks, which make all things else
Beauteous and glad, might kill the fiend within you.
Why is she barred from all society
But her own strange and uncomplaining wrongs?
Talk with me, Count, - you know I mean you well.
I stood beside your dark and fiery youth
Watching its bold and bad career, as men
Watch meteors, but it vanished not - I marked
Your desperate and remorseless manhood; now
Do I behold you in dishonoured age
Charged with a thousand unrepented crimes.
Yet I have ever hoped you would amend,
And in that hope have saved your life three times.

Cen. For which Aldobrandino owes you now
My fief beyond the Pincian. - Cardinal,
One thing, I pray you, recollect henceforth,
And so we shall converse with less restraint.
A man you knew spoke of my wife and daughter -
He was accustomed to frequent my house;
So the next day *his* wife and daughter came
And asked if I had seen him; and I smiled:
I think they never saw him any more.

Cam. Thou execrable man, beware! -
Cen. Of thee?
Nay this is idle: - We should know each other.
As to my character for what men call crime
Seeing I please my senses as I list,
And vindicate that right with force or guile,
It is a public matter, and I care not
If I discuss it with you. I may speak

Alike to you and my own conscious heart —
For you give out that you have half reformed me,
Therefore strong vanity will keep you silent
If fear should not; both will, I do not doubt.
All men delight in sensual luxury,
All men enjoy revenge; and most exult
Over the tortures they can never feel —
Flattering their secret peace with other's pain.
But I delight in nothing else. I love
The sight of agony, and the sense of joy,
When this shall be another's, and that mine.
And I have no remorse and little fear,
Which are, I think, the checks of other men.
This mood has grown upon me, untill now
Any design my captious fancy makes
The picture of its wish, and it forms none
But such as men like you would start to know,
Is as my natural food and rest debarred
Untill it be accomplished
    Cam.   Art thou not
Most miserable?
    Cen. Why, miserable? —
No. — I am what your theologians call
Hardened; — which they must be in impudence,
So to revile a man's peculiar taste.
True, I was happier than I am, while yet
Manhood remained to act the thing I thought;
While lust was sweeter than revenge; and now
Invention palls: — Aye, we must all grow old —
But that there yet remains a deed to act

Whose horror might make sharp an appetite
Duller than mine - I'd do, - I know not what.
When I was young I thought of nothing else
But pleasure; and I fed on honey sweets:
Men, by St. Thomas! cannot live like bees
And I grew tired: - yet, till I killed a foe,
And heard his groans, and heard his childrens groans,
Knew I not what delight was else on earth,
Which now delights me little. I the rather
Look on such pangs as terror ill conceals,
The dry fixed eye ball; the pale quivering lip,
Which tell me that the spirit weeps within
Tears bitterer than the bloody sweat of Christ.
I rarely kill the body which preserves,
Like a strong prison, the soul within my power,
Wherein I feed it with the breath of fear
For hourly pain.

Cam.   Hell's most abandoned fiend
Did never, in the drunkenness of guilt,
Speak to his heart as now you speak to me,
I thank my God that I believe you not.

Enter ANDREA.

Andr. My Lord, a gentleman from Salamanca
Would speak with you.

Cen. Bid him attend me in the grand saloon.
(Exit ANDR.)

Cam. Farewell; and I will pray
Almighty God that thy false, impious words
Tempt not his spirit to abandon thee
(Exit CAMILLO)

Cen. The third of my possessions! I must use
Close husbandry, or gold, the old man's sword,
Falls from my withered hand. But yesterday
There came an order from the Pope to make
Fourfold provision for my cursed sons;
Whom I have sent from Rome to Salamanca,
Hoping some accident might cut them off;
And meaning if I could to starve them there.
I pray thee, God, send some quick death upon them!
Bernardo and my wife could not be worse
If dead and damned: – then, as to Beatrice –
        (*looking around him suspiciously*)
I think they cannot hear me at that door;
What if they should? And yet I need not speak
Though the heart triumphs with itself in words.
O, thou most silent air, that shall not hear
What now I think! Thou, pavement, which I tread
Towards her chamber, – let your echoes talk
Of my imperious step scorning surprise,
But not of my intent! – Andrea!

          Enter ANDREA.

And. My lord?
Cen. Bid Beatrice attend me in her chamber
This evening: – no, at midnight and alone.

                (*Exeunt*)

SCENE II.

A garden of the Cenci Palace
Enter BEATRICE *and* ORSINO , *as in conversation.*

Beatr. Pervert not truth,
Orsino. You remember where we held
That conversation; – nay, we see the spot
Even from this cypress; – two long years are past
Since, on an April midnight, underneath
The moon-light ruins of mount Palatine,
I did confess to you my secret mind.
Ors. You said you loved me then.
Beatr. You are a Priest,
Speak to me not of love.
Ors. I may obtain
The dispensation of the Pope to marry.
Because I am a Priest do you believe
Your image , as the hunter some struck deer,
Follows me not whether I wake or sleep?
Beatr. As I have said, speak to me not of love;
Had you a dispensation I have not;
Nor will I leave this home of misery
Whilst my poor Bernard , and that gentle lady
To whom I owe life, and these virtuous thoughts,
Must suffer what I still have strength to share.
Alas, Orsino! All the love that once
I felt for you, is turned to bitter pain.
Our's was a youthful contract, which you first
Broke , by assuming vows no Pope will loose.
                                          2

And yet I love you still, but holily,
Even as a sister or a spirit might;
And so I swear a cold fidelity.
And it is well perhaps we shall not marry.
You have a sly, equivocating vein
That suits me not. – Ah, wretched that I am!
Where shall I turn? Even now you look on me
As you were not my friend, and as if you
Discovered that I thought so, with false smiles
Making my true suspicion seem your wrong.
Ah! No, forgive me; sorrow makes me seem
Sterner than else my nature might have been;
I have a weight of melancholy thoughts,
And they forbode, – but what can they forbode
Worse than I now endure?

   Ors. All will be well.
Is the petition yet prepared? You know
My zeal for all you wish, sweet Beatrice;
Doubt not but I will use my utmost skill
So that the Pope attend to your complaint.

   Beatr. Your zeal for all I wish; – Ah me, you
      are cold!
Your utmost skill . . . speak but one word . . .
                    (*aside*) Alas!
Weak and deserted creature that I am,
Here I stand bickering with my only friend!
           (*To* ORSINO)
This night my father gives a sumptuous feast,
Orsino; he has heard some happy news
From Salamanca, from my brothers there,

And with this outward shew of love he mocks
His inward hate. 'Tis bold hypocrisy
For he would gladlier celebrate their deaths,
Which I have heard him pray for on his knees:
Great God! that such a father should be mine!
But there is mighty preparation made,
And all our kin, the Cenci, will be there,
And all the chief nobility of Rome.
And he has bidden me and my pale Mother
Attire ourselves in festival array.
Poor lady! She expects some happy change
In his dark spirit from this act; I none.
At supper I will give you the petition:
'Till when - farewell.

    Ors. Farewell.

              (*Exit* BEATRICE.)

                        I know the Pope
Will ne'er absolve me from my priestly vow
But by absolving me from the revenue
Of many a wealthy see; and, Beatrice,
I think to win thee at an easier rate.
Nor shall he read her eloquent petition:
He might bestow her on some poor relation
Of his sixth cousin, as he did her sister,
And I should be debarred from all access.
Then as to what she suffers from her father,
In all this there is much exaggeration: -
Old men are testy and will have their way;
A man may stab his enemy, or his slave,
And live a free life as to wine or women,

And with a peevish temper may return
To a dull home, and rate his wife and children;
Daughters and wives call this, foul tyranny.
I shall be well content if on my conscience
There rest no heavier sin than what they suffer
From the devices of my love - A net
From which she shall escape not. Yet I fear
Her subtle mind, her awe - inspiring gaze,
Whose beams anatomize me nerve by nerve
And lay me bare, and make me blush to see
My hidden thoughts. - Ah, no! A friendless girl
Who clings to me, as to her only hope: -
I were a fool, not less than if a panther
Were panic-stricken by the Antelope's eye
If she escape me.

> (*Exit*)

SCENE III.

A magnificent Hall in the Cenci Palace.
A Banquet. Enter CENCI, LUCRETIA, BEATRICE,
ORSINO, CAMILLO, NOBLES.

Cen. Welcome, my friends and Kinsmen; wel-
　　　come ye,
Princes and Cardinals, pillars of the church,
Whose presence honours our festivity.
I have too long lived like an Anchorite,
And in my absence from your merry meetings
An evil word is gone abroad of me;

But I do hope that you, my noble friends,
When you have shared the entertainment here,
And heard the pious cause for which 'tis given,
And we have pledged a health or two together,
Will think me flesh and blood as well as you;
Sinful indeed, for Adam made all so,
But tender - hearted, meek and pitiful.

    1. *Guest.* In truth, my Lord, you seem too
        light of heart,
Too sprightly and companionable a man,
To act the deeds that rumour pins on you.
                (*To his companion*)
I never saw such blithe and open cheer
In any eye!

    2. *Guest.* Some most desired event,
In which we all demand a common joy,
Has brought us hither; let us hear it, Count.

    Cen. It is indeed a most desired event.
If when a parent from a parent's heart
Lifts from this earth to the great father of all
A prayer, both when he lays him down to sleep,
And when he rises up from dreaming it;
One supplication, one desire, one hope,
That he would grant a wish for his two sons
Even all that he demands in their regard –
And suddenly beyond his dearest hope,
It is accomplished, he should then rejoice,
And call his friends and kinsmen to a feast,
And task their love to grace his merriment,
Then honour me thus far - for I am he.

Beatr. (*to Lucretia*) Great God ! How horrible!
    Some dreadful ill
Must have befallen my brothers.
    Lucr. Fear not, Child,
He speaks too frankly.
    Beatr. Ah ! My blood runs cold.
I fear that wicked laughter round his eye
Which wrinkles up the skin even to the hair.
    Cen. Here are the letters brought from Sala-
        manca ;
Beatrice, read them to your mother. God!
I thank thee! In one night didst thou perform,
By ways inscrutable, the thing I sought.
My disobedient and rebellious sons
Are dead ! - Why dead ! - What means this change
        of cheer?
You hear me not, I tell you they are dead ;
And they will need no food or raiment more:
The tapers that did light them the dark way
Are their last cost. The Pope, I think, will not
Expect I should maintain them in their coffins.
Rejoice with me - my heart is wondrous glad.
    Beatr. (*Lucretia sinks , half fainting; Beatrice
        supports her.*)
It is not true ! - Dear lady, pray look up.
Had it been true, there is a God in Heaven,
He would not live to boast of such a boon.
Unnatural man, thou knowest that it is false.
    Cen. Aye, as the word of God; whom here I call
To witness that I speak the sober truth ; -

And whose most favouring Providence was shewn
Even in the manner of their deaths. For Rocco
Was kneeling at the mass, with sixteen others,
When the Church fell and crushed him to a mummy,
The rest escaped unhurt. Cristofano
Was stabbed in error by a jealous man,
Whilst she he loved was sleeping with his rival;
All in the self same hour of the same night;
Which shews that Heaven has special care of me.
I beg those friends who love me, that they mark
The day a feast upon their calenders.
It was the twenty seventh of December:
Aye, read the letters if you doubt my oath.
(*the assembly appears confused; several of the guests
     rise*).
  1. *Guest.* Oh, horrible! I will depart.—
  2. *Guest.* And I.—
  3. *Guest.* No, stay!
I do believe it is some jest; tho' faith!
'Tis mocking us somewhat too solemnly.
I think his son has married the Infanta,
Or found a mine of gold in El dorado;
'Tis but to season some such news; stay, stay!
I see 'tis only raillery by his smile.
    Cen. (*filling a bowl of wine, and lifting it up*)
Oh, thou bright wine whose purple splendor leaps
And bubbles gaily in this golden bowl
Under the lamp light, as my spirits do,
To hear the death of my accursed sons!
Could I believe thou wert their mingled blood,

Then would I taste thee like a sacrament,
And pledge with thee the mighty Devil in Hell,
Who, if a father's curses, as men say,
Climb with swift wings after their childrens souls,
And drag them from the very throne of Heaven,
Now triumphs in my triumph!- But thou art
Superfluous; I have drunken deep of joy
And I will taste no other wine to night.
Here, Andrea! Bear the bowl around.

 A Guest (*rising*) Thou wretch!
Will none among this noble company
Check the abandoned villain?

 Cam. For God's sake
Let me dismiss the guests! You are insane,
Some ill will come of this .

 2. *Guest* Seize, silence him!

 1. *Guest* I will!

 3. *Guest* And I!

 Cen. (*Addressing those who rise with a threatening*
   gesture)
Who moves? Who speaks?

    (*Turning to the Company*)
       'tis nothing,
Enjoy yourselves .- Beware! For my revenge
Is as the sealed commission of a king
That kills, and none dare name the murderer.

  (*The Banquet is broken up; several of the*
   Guests are departing.

 Beatr. I do entreat you, go not, noble guests;
What although tyranny, and impious hate

Stand sheltered by a father's hoary hair?
What, if 'tis he who clothed us in these limbs
Who tortures them, and triumphs? What, if we,
The desolate and the dead, were his own flesh,
His children and his wife, whom he is bound
To love and shelter? Shall we therefore find
No refuge in this merciless wide world?
Oh, think what deep wrongs must have blotted out
First love, then reverence in a child's prone mind
Till it thus vanquish shame and fear! O, think
I have borne much, and kissed the sacred hand
Which crushed us to the earth, and thought
     its stroke
Was perhaps some paternal chastisement!
Have excused much, doubted; and when no doubt
Remained, have sought by patience, love and tears
To soften him, and when this could not be
I have knelt down through the long sleepless nights
And lifted up to God, the father of all,
Passionate prayers: and when these were not heard
I have still borne, - until I meet you here,
Princes and kinsmen, at this hideous feast
Given at my brothers' deaths. Two yet remain,
His wife remains and I, whom if ye save not,
Ye may soon share such merriment again
As fathers make over their childrens graves.
Oh! Prince Colonna, thou art our near kinsman,
Cardinal, thou art the Pope's chamberlain,
Camillo, thou art chief justiciary,
Take us away!

         3

Cen. (*He has been conversing with Camillo*
during the first part of Beatrice' s speech ;
he hears the conclusion, and now advances.
I hope my good friends here
Will think of their own daughters - or perhaps
Of their own throats - before they lend an ear
To this wild girl.

    Beatr. (*Not noticing the words of Cenci.*)
Dare not one look on me ?
None answer ? Can one tyrant overbear
The sense of many best and wisest men ?
Or is it that I sue not in some form
Of scrupulous law, that ye deny my suit ?
Oh, God ! That I were buried with my brothers!
And that the flowers of this departed spring
Were fading on my grave ! And that my father
Were celebrating now one feast for all !

    Cam. A bitter wish for one so young and gentle;
Can we do nothing ? -

    Colon. Nothing that I see.
Count Cenci were a dangerous enemy:
Yet I would second any one.

    A Card. And I.

    Cen. Retire to your chamber, insolent girl!

    Beatr. Retire thou impious man ! Aye hide thyself
Where never eye can look upon thee more !
Wouldst thou have honour and obedience
Who art a torturer ? Father, never dream
Though thou mayst overbear this company,
But ill must come of ill. - Frown not on me !

Haste hide thyself, lest with avenging looks
My brothers'ghosts should hunt thee from thy seat!
Cover thy face from every living eye,
And start if thou but hear a human step:
Seek out some dark and silent corner, there,
Bow thy white head before offended God,
And we will kneel around, and fervently
Pray that he pity both ourselves and thee.

Cen. My friends, I do lament this insane girl
Has spoilt the mirth of our festivity.
Good night, farewell; I will not make you longer
Spectators of our dull domestic quarrels.
Another time. –

    (*Exeunt all but* CENCI *and* BEATRICE)
    My brain is swimming round;
Give me a bowl of wine!
   (*To* BEATRICE) Thou painted viper!
Beast that thou art! Fair and yet terrible!
I know a charm shall make thee meek and tame,
Now get thee from my sight!

      (*Exit* BEATRICE)
    Here, Andrea,
Fill up this goblet with Greek wine. I said
I would not drink this evening; but I must;
For, strange to say, I feel my spirits fail
With thinking what I have decreed to do. –
     (*Drinking the wine*)
Be thou the resolution of quick youth

Within my veins, and manhood's purpose stern,
And age's firm, cold, subtle villainy;
As if thou wert indeed my children's blood
Which I did thirst to drink! The charm works
    well;
It must be done; it shall be done, I swear!

(Exit)

END OF THE FIRST ACT.

A C T II.

SCENE I.

An apartment in the Cenci Palace.
Enter LUCRETIA *and* BERNARDO.

Lucr. Weep not, my gentle boy; he struck
    but me
Who have borne deeper wrongs. In truth, if he
Had killed me, he had done a kinder deed.
O, God Almighty, do thou look upon us,
We have no other friend but only thee!
Yet weep not; though I love you as my own
I am not your true mother.
    Ber. Oh more, more,
Than ever mother was to any child,
That have you been to me! Had he not been
My father, do you think that I should weep?
    Lucr. Alas! Poor boy, what else could'st thou
    have done?
            Enter BEATRICE.
    Beatr. (*In a hurried voice*)
Did he pass this way? Have you seen him,
    brother?
Ah! No, that is his step upon the stairs;
'Tis nearer now; his hand is on the door;
Mother, if I to thee have ever been

A duteous child, now save me! Thou, great God,
Whose image upon earth a father is,
Dost thou indeed abandon me! He comes;
The door is opening now; I see his face;
He frowns on others, but he smiles on me,
Even as he did after the feast last night.

Enter a Servant.

Almighty God, how merciful thou art!
'Tis but Orsino's servant. - Well, what news?
   Serv. My master bids me say, the Holy Father
Has sent back your petition thus unopened.

(*Giving a paper*)

And he demands at what hour 'twere secure
To visit you again?
   Lucr. At the Ave Mary.

(*Exit Servant.*)

So, daughter, our last hope has failed; Ah me!
How pale you look; you tremble, and you stand
Wrapped in some fixed and fearful meditation,
As if one thought were over strong for you:
Your eyes have a chill glare; O, dearest child!
Are you gone mad? If not, pray speak to me.
   Beatr. You see I am not mad; I speak to you.
   Lucr. You talked of some thing that your fa-
         ther did
After that dreadful feast? Could it be worse
Than when he smiled, and cried, My sons are dead!
And every one looked in his neighbour's face
To see if others were as white as he?
At the first word he spoke I felt the blood

Rush to my heart, and fell into a trance;
And when it past I sat all weak and wild;
Whilst you alone stood up, and with strong words
Checked his unnatural pride; and I could see
The devil was rebuked that lives in him.
Until this hour thus you have ever stood
Between us and your father's moody wrath
Like a protecting presence: your firm mind
Has been our only refuge and defence:
What can have thus subdued it? What can now
Have given you that cold melancholy look,
Succeeding to your unaccustomed fear?

    Beatr. What is it that you say? I was just
        thinking
'Twere better not to struggle any more.
Men, like my father, have been dark and bloody,
Yet never - O! Before worse comes of it
'Twere wise to die: it ends in that at last.

    Lucr. Oh, talk not so, dear child! Tell me at
        once
What did your father do or say to you?
He stayed not after that accursed feast
One moment in your chamber. - Speak to me.

    Ber. Oh, sister, sister, prithee, speak to us!

    Beatr. (*Speaking very slowly with a forced*
        calmness)
It was one word, Mother, one little word;
One look, one smile. (*wildly*)
                Oh! He has trampled me
Under his feet, and made the blood stream down

My pallid cheeks. And he has given us all
Ditch water, and the fever-stricken flesh
Of buffaloes, and bade us eat or starve,
And we have eaten. – He has made me look
On my beloved Bernardo, when the rust
Of heavy chains has gangrened his sweet limbs,
And I have never yet despaired – but now!
What would I say?

                  (*recovering herself.*)
           Ah! No, 'tis nothing new.
The sufferings we all share have made me wild:
He only struck and cursed me as he passed;
He said, he looked, he did; – nothing at all
Beyond his wont, yet it disordered me.
Alas! I am forgetful of my duty,
I should preserve my senses for your sake.
    Lucr. Nay, Beatrice; have courage my sweet girl.
If any one despairs it should be I
Who loved him once, and now must live with him
Till God in pity call for him or me.
For you may, like your sister, find some husband,
And smile, years hence, with children round your
         knees;
Whilst I, then dead, and all this hideous coil
Shall be remembered only as a dream.
    Beatr. Talk not to me, dear lady, of a husband.
Did you not nurse me when my mother died?
Did you not shield me and that dearest boy?
And had we any other friend but you
In infancy, with gentle words and looks,

To win our father not to murder us?
And shall I now desert you? May the ghost
Of my dead Mother plead against my soul
If I abandon her who filled the place
She left, with more, even, than a mother's love!

Ber. And I am of my sister's mind. Indeed
I would not leave you in this wretchedness,
Even though the Pope should make me free
     to live
In some blithe place, like others of my age,
With sports, and delicate food, and the fresh air,
Oh, never think that I will leave you, Mother!

Lucr. My dear, dear children!

     Enter CENCI, *suddenly.*

Cen. What, Beatrice here!
Come hither! (*she shrinks back, and covers her face*)
     Nay hide not your face, 'tis fair;
Look up! Why, yesternight you dared to look
With disobedient insolence upon me,
Bending a stern and an inquiring brow
On what I meant; whilst I then sought to hide
That which I came to tell you - but in vain.

Beatr. (*Wildly, staggering towards the door.*)
Oh, that the earth would gape! Hide me, oh God!

Cen. Then it was I whose inarticulate words
Fell from my lips, and who with tottering steps
Fled from your presence, as you now from mine.
Stay, I command you - from this day and hour
Never again, I think, with fearless eye,
And brow superior, and unaltered cheek,

     4

And that lip made for tenderness or scorn,
Shalt thou strike dumb the meanest of mankind;
Me least of all. Now get thee to thy chamber!
Thou too, loathed image of thy cursed mother,
                    (*to* BERNARDO)
Thy milky, meek face makes me sick with hate!
            (*Exeunt* BEATR. *and* BER.)
   (*Aside.*) So much has past between us as must
        make
Me bold, her fearful. - 'Tis an awful thing
To touch such mischief as I now conceive:
So men sit shivering on the dewy bank,
And try the chill stream with their feet; once in ...
How the delighted spirit pants for joy!
   Lucr. (*Advancing timidly towards him*)
Oh, husband! Pray forgive poor Beatrice,
She meant not any ill.
   Cen. Nor you perhaps?
Nor that young imp, whom you have taught
        by rote
Parricide with his alphabet? Nor Giacomo?
Nor those two most unnatural sons, who stirred
Enmity up against me with the Pope?
Whom in one night merciful God cut off:
Innocent lambs! They thought not any ill.
You were not here conspiring? You said nothing
Of how I might be dungeoned as a madman;
Or be condemned to death for some offence,
And you would be the witnesses? - This failing,
How just it were to hire assassins, or

Put sudden poison in my evening drink?
Or smother me when overcome by wine?
Seeing we had no other judge but God,
And he had sentenced me, and there were none
But you to be the executioners
Of his decree enregistered in heaven?
Oh, no! You said not this?

    Lucr. So help me God,
I never thought the things you charge me with!

    Cen. If you dare speak that wicked lie again
I'll kill you. What! It was not by your counsel
That Beatrice disturbed the feast last night?
You did not hope to stir some enemies
Against me, and escape, and laugh to scorn
What every nerve of you now trembles at?
You judged that men were bolder than they are;
Few dare to stand between their grave and me.

    Lucr. Look not so dreadfully! By my salvation
I knew not aught that Beatrice designed;
Nor do I think she designed any thing
Until she heard you talk of her dead brothers.

    Cen. Blaspheming liar! You are damned for
    this!
But I will take you where you may persuade
The stones you tread on to deliver you:
For men shall there be none but those who dare
All things – not question that which I command.
On Wednesday next I shall set out: you know
That savage rock, the Castle of Petrella,
'Tis safely walled, and moated round about:

Its dungeons underground, and its thick towers
Never told tales; though they have heard and seen
What might make dumb things speak. - Why
    do you linger ?
Make speediest preparation for the journey!

(*Exit* LUCRETIA)

The all beholding sun yet shines; I hear
A busy stir of men about the streets;
I see the bright sky through the window panes;
It is a garish, broad, and peering day;
Loud, light, suspicious, full of eyes and ears,
And every little corner, nook and hole
Is penetrated with the insolent light.
Come darkness! Yet, what is the day to me?
And wherefore should I wish for night, who do
A deed which shall confound both night and day?
'Tis she shall grope through a bewildering mist
Of horror: if there be a sun in heaven
She shall not dare to look upon its beams;
Nor feel its warmth. Let her then wish for night;
The act I think shall soon extinguish all
For me: I bear a darker deadlier gloom
Than the earth's shade, or interlunar air,
Or constellations quenched in murkiest cloud,
In which I walk secure and unbeheld
Towards my purpose. - Would that it were done!

(*Exit.*)

SCENE II.

A chamber in the Vatican.
Enter CAMILLO *and* GIACOMO, *in conversation.*

Cam. There is an obsolete and doubtful law
By which you might obtain a bare provision
Of food and clothing –
    Giac. Nothing more? Alas!
Bare must be the provision which strict law
Awards, and aged, sullen avarice pays.
Why did my father not apprentice me
To some mechanic trade? I should have then
Been trained in no highborn necessities
Which I could meet not by my daily toil.
The eldest son of a rich nobleman
Is heir to all his incapacities;
He has wide wants, and narrow powers. If you,
Cardinal Camillo, were reduced at once
From thrice-driven beds of down, and delicate food,
An hundred servants, and six palaces,
To that which nature doth indeed require? –
    Cam. Nay, there is reason in your plea;
       'twere hard.
    Giac. 'Tis hard for a firm man to bear: but I
Have a dear wife, a lady of high birth,
Whose dowry in ill hour I lent my father
Without a bond or witness to the deed:
And children, who inherit her fine senses,
The fairest creatures in this breathing world;

And she and they reproach me not. Cardinal,
Do you not think the Pope would interpose
And stretch authority beyond the law?

Cam. Though your peculiar case is hard, I know
The Pope will not divert the course of law.
After that impious feast the other night
I spoke with him, and urged him then to check
Your father's cruel hand; he frowned and said,
» Children are disobedient, and they sting
» Their father's hearts to madness and despair
» Requiting years of care with contumely.
» I pity the Count Cenci from my heart;
» His outraged love perhaps awakened hate,
» And thus he is exasperated to ill.
» In the great war between the old and young
» I, who have white hairs and a tottering body,
» Will keep at least blameless neutrality. »

Enter ORSINO.

You, my good lord Orsino, heard those words.

Ors. What words?

Giac. Alas, repeat them not again!
There then is no redress for me, at least
None but that which I may atchieve myself,
Since I am driven to the brink. - But, say,
My innocent sister and my only brother
Are dying underneath my father's eye.
The memorable torturers of this land,
Galeaz Visconti, Borgia, Ezzelin,
Never inflicted on their meanest slave
What these endure; shall they have no protection?

Cam. Why, if they would petition to the Pope
I see not how he could refuse it ◄ yet
He holds it of most dangerous example
In aught to weaken the paternal power,
Being, as 'twere, the shadow of his own.
I pray you now excuse me. I have business
That will not bear delay.   (*Exit* CAMILLO)
      Giac. But you, Orsino,
Have the petition wherefore not present it?
      Ors. I have presented it, and backed it with
My earnest prayers, and urgent interest;
It was returned unanswered. I doubt not
But that the strange and execrable deeds
Alledged in it - in truth they might well baffle
Any belief - have turned the Pope's displeasure
Upon the accusers from the criminal:
So I should guess from what Camillo said.
      Giac. My friend, that palace-walking devil Gold
Has whispered silence to his Holiness:
And we are left, as scorpions ringed with fire,
What should we do but strike ourselves to death?
For he who is our murderous persecutor
Is shielded by a father's holy name,
Or I would -   (*stops abruptly*)
      Ors. What? Fear not to speak your thought.
Words are but holy as the deeds they cover:
A priest who has forsworn the God he serves;
A judge who makes the truth weep at his decree;
A friend who should weave counsel, as I now,
But as the mantle of some selfish guile;

A father who is all a tyrant seems,
Were the prophaner for his sacred name.
   Giac. Ask me not what I think; the unwilling
      brain
Feigns often what it would not; and we trust
Imagination with such phantasies
As the tongue dares not fashion into words,
Which have no words, their horror makes them dim
To the mind's eye. - My heart denies itself
To think what you demand.
   Ors. But a friend's bosom
Is as the inmost cave of our own mind
Where we sit shut from the wide gaze of day,
And from the all-communicating air.
You look what I suspected -
   Giac. Spare me now!
I am as one lost in a midnight wood
Who dares not ask some harmless passenger
The path across the wilderness, lest he,
As my thoughts are, should be - a murderer.
I know you are my friend, and all I dare
Speak to my soul that will I trust with thee.
But now my heart is heavy and would take
Lone counsel from a night of sleepless care.
Pardon me, that I say farewell - farewell!
I would that to my own suspected self
I could address a word so full of peace.
   Ors. Farewell! - Be your thoughts better or
      more bold.
                  (*Exit* GIACOMO.)

I had disposed the Cardinal Camillo
To feed his hope with cold encouragement:
It fortunately serves my close designs
That 'tis a trick of this same family
To analyse their own and other minds.
Such self-anatomy shall teach the will
Dangerous secrets: for it tempts our powers,
Knowing what must be thought, and may be done,
Into the depth of darkest purposes:
So Cenci fell into the pit; even I,
Since Beatrice unveiled me to myself,
And made me shrink from what I cannot shun,
Shew a poor figure to my own esteem,
To which I grow half reconciled . I'll do
As little mischief as I can; that thought
Shall fee the accuser conscience.

                         (*After a pause*)
                Now what harm
If Cenci should be murdered? – Yet, if murdered,
Wherefore by me? And what if I could take
The profit, yet omit the sin and peril
In such an action? Of all earthly things
I fear a man whose blows outspeed his words;
And such is Cenci: and while Cenci lives
His daughter's dowry were a secret grave
If a priest wins her. – Oh, fair Beatrice!
Would that I loved thee not, or loving thee
Could but despise danger and gold and all
That frowns between my wish and its effect,
Or smiles beyond it! There is no escape ...

                         5

Her bright form kneels beside me at the altar,
And follows me to the resort of men,
And fills my slumber with tumultuous dreams,
So when I wake my blood seems liquid fire;
And if I strike my damp and dizzy head
My hot palm scorches it: her very name,
But spoken by a stranger, makes my heart
Sicken and pant; and thus unprofitably
I clasp the phantom of unfelt delights
Till weak imagination half possesses
The self created shadow. Yet much longer
Will I not nurse this life of feverous hours:
From the unravelled hopes of Giacomo
I must work out my own dear purposes.
I see, as from a tower, the end of all:
Her father dead; her brother bound to me
By a dark secret, surer than the grave;
Her mother scared and unexpostulating
From the dread manner of her wish atchieved:
And she! - Once more take courage my faint heart;
What dares a friendless maiden matched with thee?
I have such foresight as assures success:
Some unbeheld divinity doth ever,
When dread events are near, stir up men's minds
To black suggestions; and he prospers best,
Not who becomes the instrument of ill,
But who can flatter the dark spirit, that makes
Its empire and its prey of other hearts
Till it become his slave ... as I will do. (*Exit.*)

END OF THE SECOND ACT.

ACT III.

SCENE I.

An apartment in the Cenci Palace.
LUCRETIA, *to her enter* BEATRICE.

Beatr. (*She enters staggering, and speaks wildly.*)
Reach me that handkerchief! – My brain is hurt;
My eyes are full of blood; just wipe them for me...
I see but indistinctly ...
   Lucr. My sweet child,
You have no wound; 'tis only a cold dew
That starts from your dear brow ...Alas! Alas!
What has befallen?
   Beatr. How comes this hair undone?
Its wandering strings must be what blind me so,
And yet I tied it fast. – O, horrible!
The pavement sinks under my feet! The walls
Spin round! I see a woman weeping there,
And standing calm and motionless, whilst I
Slide giddily as the world reels .... My God!
The beautiful blue heaven is flecked with blood!
The sunshine on the floor is black! The air
Is changed to vapours such as the dead breathe
In charnel pits! Pah! I am choked! There creeps
A clinging, black, contaminating mist
About me ... 'tis substantial, heavy, thick,

I cannot pluck it from me, for it glues
My fingers and my limbs to one another,
And eats into my sinews, and dissolves
My flesh to a pollution, poisoning
The subtle, pure, and inmost spirit of life!
My God! I never knew what the mad felt
Before; for I am mad beyond all doubt!
                              (*more wildly*)
No, I am dead! These putrefying limbs
Shut round and sepulchre the panting soul
Which would burst forth into the wandering air!
                              (*a pause*)
What hideous thought was that I had even now?
'Tis gone; and yet its burthen remains here
O'er these dull eyes... upon this weary heart!
O, world! O, life! O, day! O, misery!
  Lucr. What ails thee, my poor child? She an-
      swers not:
Her spirit apprehends the sense of pain,
But not its cause; suffering has dried away
The source from which it sprung...
    Beatr. (*franticly*)Like Parricide ...
Misery has killed its father: yet its father
Never like mine ... O, God! What thing am I?
  Lucr. My dearest child, what has your father
      done ?
    Beatr. (*doubtfully*)
Who art thou questioner? I have no father.
                              (*aside*)
She is the madhouse nurse who tends on me

It is a piteous office.
        (*to Lucretia, in a slow, subdued voice*)
                Do you know
I thought I was that wretched Beatrice
Men speak of, whom her father sometimes hales
From hall to hall by the entangled hair;
At others, pens up naked in damp cells
Where scaly reptiles crawl, and starves her there,
Till she will eat strange flesh. This woful story
So did I overact in my sick dreams,
That I imagined ... no, it cannot be!
Horrible things have been in this wild world,
Prodigious mixtures, and confusions strange
Of good and ill; and worse have been conceived
Than ever there was found a heart to do.
But never fancy imaged such a deed
As...
        (*pauses, suddenly recollecting herself*)
Who art thou? Swear to me, ere I die
With fearful expectation, that indeed
Thou art not what thou seemest... Mother!
   Lucr. Oh!
My sweet child, know you ...
   Beatr. Yet speak it not:
For then if this be truth, that other too
Must be a truth, a firm enduring truth,
Linked with each lasting circumstance of life,
Never to change, never to pass away.
Why so it is. This is the Cenci palace;
Thou art Lucretia; I am Beatrice.

I have talked some wild words, but will no more,
Mother, come near me: from this point of time,
I am ...   (*her voice dies away faintly*)
  Lucr. Alas! What has befallen thee, child?
What has thy father done?
  Beatr. What have I done?
Am I not innocent? Is it my crime
That one with white hair, and imperious brow,
Who tortured me from my forgotten years,
As parents only dare, should call himself
My father, yet should be! – Oh, what am I?
What name, what place, what memory shall be
          mine?
What retrospects, outliving even despair?
  Lucr. He is a violent tyrant, surely, child:
We know that death alone can make us free;
His death or ours. But what can he have done
Of deadlier outrage or worse injury?
Thou art unlike thyself; thine eyes shoot forth
A wandering and strange spirit. Speak to me,
Unlock those pallid hands whose fingers twine
With one another.
  Beatr. 'Tis the restless life
Tortured within them. If I try to speak
I shall go mad. Aye, something must be done;
What, yet I know not... something which
          shall make
The thing that I have suffered but a shadow
In the dread lightning which avenges it;
Brief, rapid, irreversible, destroying

The consequence of what it cannot cure.
Some such thing is to be endured or done:
When I know what, I shall be still and calm,
And never any thing will move me more
But now! - Oh blood, which art my father's blood,
Circling thro'these contaminated veins
If thou, poured forth on the polluted earth,
Could wash away the crime, and punishment
By which I suffer.... no, that cannot be!
Many might doubt there were a God above
Who sees and permits evil, and so die:
That faith no agony shall obscure in me.

    Lucr. It must indeed have been some bitter
        wrong ;
Yet what, I dare not guess: Oh, my lost child,
Hide not in proud impenetrable grief
Thy sufferings from my fear.

    Beatr. I hide them not.
What are the words which you would have me
        speak ?
I, who can feign no image in my mind
Of that which has transformed me. I, whose
        thought
Is like a ghost shrouded and folded up
In its own formless horror. Of all words,
That minister to mortal intercourse,
Which wouldst thou hear? For there is none
        to tell
My misery: if another ever knew
Aught like to it, she died as I will die.

And left it, as I must, without a name.
Death! Death! Our law and our religion call thee
A punishment and a reward ... Oh, which
Have I deserved?
    Lucr. The peace of innocence;
Till in your season you be called to heaven.
Whate'er you may have suffered, you have done
No evil. Death must be the punishment
Of crime, or the reward of trampling down
The thorns which God has strewed upon the path
Which leads to immortality.
Beatr. Aye, death ...
The punishment of crime. I pray thee, God,
Let me not be bewildered while I judge.
If I must live day after day, and keep
These limbs, the unworthy temple of thy spirit,
As a foul den from which what thou abhorrest
May mock thee, unavenged ... it shall not be!
Self murder ... no that might be no escape,
For thy decree yawns like a Hell between
Our will and it: – O! In this mortal world
There is no vindication and no law
Which can adjudge and execute the doom
Of that through which I suffer.
               Enter ORSINO
(*She approaches him solemnly*) Welcome, Friend!
I have to tell you that, since last we met,
I have endured a wrong so great and strange,
That neither life or death can give me rest.
Ask me not what it is, for there are deeds

Which have no form, sufferings which have no
    tongue.
  Ors. And what is he who has thus injured you?
  Beatr. The man they call my father: a dread
    name.
  Ors. It cannot be...
  Beatr. What it can be, or not,
Forbear to think. It is, and it has been;
Advise me how it shall not be again.
I thought to die; but a religious awe
Restrains me, and the dread lest death itself
Might be no refuge from the consciousness
Of what is yet unexpiated. Oh, speak!
  Ors. Accuse him of the deed, and let the law
Avenge thee.
  Beatr. Oh, ice-hearted counsellor!
If I could find a word that might make known
The crime of my destroyer; and that done
My tongue should like a knife tear out the secret
Which cankers my heart's core; aye, lay all bare
So that my unpolluted fame should be
With vilest gossips a stale mouthed story;
A mock, a bye-word, an astonishment: -
If this were done, which never shall be done,
Think of the offender's gold, his dreaded hate,
And the strange horror of the accuser's tale,
Baffling belief, and overpowering speech;
Scarce whispered, unimaginable, wrapt
In hideous hints... Oh, most assured redress!
  Ors. You will endure it then?
             6

Beatr. Endure ? - Orsino,
It seems your counsel is small profit.
(*Turns from him, and speaks half to herself*)
                                    Aye,
All must be suddenly resolved and done.
What is this undistinguishable mist.
Of thoughts, which rise, like shadow after
        shadow,
Darkening each other?
    Ors. Should the offender live ?
Triumph in his misdeed? and make, by use,
His crime, whate'er it is, dreadful no doubt,
Thine element; until thou mayest become
Utterly lost; subdued even to the hue
Of that which thou permittest?
    Beatr. (*To herself*) Mighty death!
Thou double visaged shadow! Only judge!
Rightfullest arbiter!
                    (*She retires absorbed in thought.*)
    Lucr. If the lightning
Of God has e'er descended to avenge ...
    Ors. Blaspheme not ! His high Providence
        commits
Its glory on this earth, and their own wrongs
Into the hands of men; if they neglect
To punish crime ...
    Lucr. But if one, like this wretch,
Should mock with gold, opinion law and power?
If there be no appeal to that which makes
The guiltiest tremble? If because our wrongs,

For that they are, unnatural, strange and mon
         strous,
Exceed all measure of belief? Oh, God!
If, for the very reasons which should make
Redress most swift and sure, our injurer triumphs?
And we the victims, bear worse punishment
Than that appointed for their torturer?

    Ors. Think not
But that there is redress where there is wrong,
So we be bold enough to seize it.

    Lucr. How?
If there were any way to make all sure,
I know not... but I think it might be good
To ...

    Ors. Why, his late outrage to Beatrice;
For it is such, as I but faintly guess,
As makes remorse dishonour, and leaves her
Only one duty, how she may avenge:
You, but one refuge from ills ill endured;
Me, but one counsel ...

    Lucr. For we cannot hope
That aid, or retribution, or resource
Will arise thence, where every other one
Might find them with less need.

        (BEATRICE *advances.*)
    Ors. Then ...
    Beatr. Peace, Orsino!
And, honoured Lady, while I speak, I pray,
That you put off, as garments overworn,
Forbearance and respect, remorse and fear,

And all the fit restraints of daily life,
Which have been borne from childhood, but
      which now
Would be a mockery to my holier plea.
As I have said, I have endured a wrong,
Which, though it be expressionless, is such
As asks atonement; both for what is past,
And lest I be reserved, day after day,
To load with crimes an overburthened soul,
And be... what ye can dream not. I have prayed
To God, and I have talked with my own heart,
And have unravelled my entangled will,
And have at length determined what is right.
Art thou my friend Orsino? False or true?
Pledge thy salvation ere I speak.
      Ors. I swear
To dedicate my cunning, and my strength
My silence, and whatever else is mine,
To thy commands.
      Lucr. You think we should devise
His death?
      Beatr. And execute what is devised,
And suddenly. We must be brief and bold.
      Ors. And yet most cautious.
      Lucr. For the jealous laws
Would punish us with death and infamy
For that which it became themselves to do.
      Beatr. Be cautious as ye may, but prompt.
         Orsino;
What are the means?

Ors. I know two dull, fierce outlaws,
Who think man's spirit as a worm's, and they
Would trample out, for any slight caprice,
The meanest or the noblest life. This mood
Is marketable here in Rome. They sell
What we now want.
    Lucr. To morrow before dawn,
Cenci will take us to that lonely rock,
Petrella, in the Apulian Appenines.
If he arrive there ...
    Beatr. He must not arrive.
    Ors. Will it be dark before you reach the tower?
    Lucr. The sun will scarce be set.
    Beatr. But I remember
Two miles on this side of the fort, the road
Crosses a deep ravine; 'tis rough and narrow,
And winds with short turns down the precipice;
And in its depth there is a mighty rock,
Which has, from unimaginable years,
Sustained itself with terror and with toil
Over a gulph, and with the agony
With which it clings seems slowly coming down;
Even as a wretched soul hour after hour,
Clings to the mass of life; yet clinging, leans;
And leaning, makes more dark the dread abyss
In which it fears to fall : beneath this crag
Huge as despair, as if in weariness,
The melancholy mountain yawns ... below,
You hear but see not an impetuous torrent
Raging among the caverns, and a bridge

Crosses the chasm; and high above there grow,
With intersecting trunks, from crag to crag,
Cedars, and yews, and pines; whosetangled hair
Is matted in one solid roof of shade
By the dark ivy's twine. At noon day here
'Tis twilight, and at sunset blackest night.

   Ors. Before you reach that bridge make some
        excuse
For spurring on your mules, or loitering
Until ...

   Beatr. What sound is that?

   Lucr. Hark! No, it cannot be a servant's step;
It must be Cenci, unexpectedly
Returned ... Make some excuse for being here.

   Beatr.   (*to* ORSINO, *as she goes out*)
That step we hear approach must never pass
The bridge of which we spoke.

            (*Exeunt* LUCRETIA *and* BEATRICE)

   Ors. What shall I do?
Cenci must find me here, and I must bear
The imperious inquisition of his looks
As to what brought me hither: let me mask
Mine own in some inane and vacant smile.

       Enter GIACOMO, *in a hurried manner.*
How! Have you ventured thither? know you then
That Cenci is from home?

   Giac. I sought him here;
And now must wait till he returns.

   Ors. Great God!
Weigh you the danger of this rashness?

Giac. Aye!
Does my destroyer know his danger? We
Are now no more, as once, parent and child,
But man to man; the oppressor to the oppressed;
The slanderer to the slandered; foe to foe:
He has cast Nature off, which was his shield,
And Nature casts him off, who is her shame;
And I spurn both. Is it a father's throat
Which I will shake, and say, I ask not gold;
I ask not happy years; nor memories
Of tranquil childhood; nor home-sheltered love;
Though all these hast thou torn from me, and more;
But only my fair fame; only one hoard
Of peace, which I thought hidden from thy hate,
Under the penury heaped on me by thee,
Or I will ... God can understand and pardon,
Why should I speak with man?

   Ors. Be calm, dear friend.

   Giac. Well, I will calmly tell you what he did.
This old Francesco Cenci, as you know,
Borrowed the dowry of my wife from me,
And then denied the loan; and left me so
In poverty, the which I sought to mend
By holding a poor office in the state.
It had been promised to me, and already
I bought new clothing for my ragged babes,
And my wife smiled; and my heart knew repose.
When Cenci's intercession, as I found,
Conferred this office on a wretch, whom thus
He paid for vilest service. I returned

With this ill news, and we sate sad together
Solacing our despondency with tears
Of such affection and unbroken faith
As temper life's worst bitterness; when he,
As he is wont, came to upbraid and curse,
Mocking our poverty, and telling us
Such was God's scourge for disobedient sons.
And then, that I might strike him dumb with shame,
I spoke of my wife's dowry; but he coined
A brief yet specious tale, how I had wasted
The sum in secret riot; and he saw
My wife was touched, and he went smiling forth.
And when I knew the impression he had made,
And felt my wife insult with silent scorn
My ardent truth, and look averse and cold,
I went forth too: but soon returned again;
Yet not so soon but that my wife had taught
My children her harsh thoughts, and they all cried,
» Give us clothes, father! Give us better food!
» What you in one night squander were enough
» For months! » I looked, and saw that home
        was hell.
And to that hell will I return no more
Until mine enemy has rendered up
Atonement, or, as he gave life to me
I will, reversing nature's law...
    Ors. Trust me,
The compensation which thou seekest here
Will be denied.
    Giac. Then... Are you not my friend?

Did you not hint at the alternative,
Upon the brink of which you see I stand,
The other day when we conversed together?
My wrongs were then less. That word parricide,
Although I am resolved, haunts me like fear.

Ors. It must be fear itself, for the bare word
Is hollow mockery. Mark, how wisest God
Draws to one point the threads of a just doom,
So sanctifying it: what you devise
Is, as it were, accomplished.

Giac. Is he dead?

Ors. His grave is ready. Know that since we met
Cenci has done an outrage to his daughter.

Giac What outrage?

Ors. That she speaks not, but you may
Conceive such half conjectures as I do,
From her fixed paleness, and the lofty grief
Of her stern brow bent on the idle air,
And her severe unmodulated voice,
Drowning both tenderness and dread; and last
From this; that whilst her step-mother and I,
Bewildered in our horror, talked together
With obscure hints; both self-misunderstood
And darkly guessing, stumbling, in our talk,
Over the truth, and yet to its revenge,
She interrupted us, and with a look
Which told before she spoke it, he must die...

Giac. It is enough . My doubts are well appeased;
There is a higher reason for the act
Than mine; there is a holier judge than me,

7

A more unblamed avenger. Beatrice,
Who in the gentleness of thy sweet youth
Hast never trodden on a worm, or bruised
A living flower, but thou hast pitied it
With needless tears! Fair sister, thou in whom
Men wondered how such loveliness and wisdom
Did not destroy each other! Is there made
Ravage of thee? O, heart, I ask no more
Justification! Shall I wait, Orsino,
Till he return, and stab him at the door?

Ors. Not so; some accident might interpose
To rescue him from what is now most sure;
And you are unprovided where to fly,
How to excuse or to conceal. Nay, listen:
All is contrived; success is so assured
That ...

Enter BEATRICE

Beatr. 'Tis my brother's voice! You know me not?
Giac. My sister, my lost sister!
Beatr. Lost indeed!
I see Orsino has talked with you, and
That you conjecture things too horrible
To speak, yet far less than the truth. Now, stay not,
He might return: yet kiss me; I shall know
That then thou hast consented to his death.
Farewell, Farewell! Let piety to God,
Brotherly love, justice and clemency,
And all things that make tender hardest hearts
Make thine hard, brother. Answer not ... farewell.
                        (*Exeunt severally*)

SCENE II.

A mean apartment in GIACOMO'S *house.*
GIACOMO, *alone.*

Giac. 'Tis midnight, and Orsino comes not yet.
           (*Thunder, and the sound of a storm.*)
What! can the everlasting elements
Feel with a worm like man? If so the shaft
Of mercy-winged lightning would not fall
On stones and trees. My wife and children sleep:
They are now living in unmeaning dreams:
But I must wake, still doubting if that deed
Be just which was most necessary. O,
Thou unreplenished lamp! whose narrow fire
Is shaken by the wind, and on whose edge
Devouring darkness hovers! Thou small flame,
Which, as a dying pulse rises and falls,
Still flickerest up and down, how very soon,
Did I not feed thee, wouldst thou fail and be
As thou hadst never been! So wastes and sinks
Even now, perhaps, the life that kindled mine:
But that no power can fill with vital oil
That broken lamp of flesh. Ha! 'tis the blood
Which fed these veins that ebbs till all is cold:
It is the form that moulded mine that sinks
Into the white and yellow spasms of death:
It is the soul by which mine was arrayed
In God's immortal likeness which now stands

Naked before Heaven's judgement seat!

(a bell strikes)

One! Two!

The hours crawl on; and when my hairs are white
My son will then perhaps be waiting thus,
Tortured between just hate and vain remorse;
Chiding the tardy messenger of news
Like those which I expect. I almost wish
He be not dead, although my wrongs are great;
Yet ... 'tis Orsino's step...

Enter ORSINO

Speak!

  Ors. I am come
To say he has escaped.
  Giac. Escaped!
  Ors. And safe
Within Petrella. He past by the spot
Appointed for the deed an hour too soon.
  Giac. Are we the fools of such contingencies?
And do we waste in blind misgivings thus
The hours when we should act? Then wind and
       thunder,
Which seemed to howl his knell, is the loud
       laughter
With which Heaven mocks our weakness! I hen-
      ceforth
Will ne'er repent of aught designed or done
But my repentance.
  Ors. See, the lamp is out.
  Giac. If no remorse is ours when the dim air

Has drank this innocent flame, why should we
      quail
When Cenci's life, that light by which ill spirits
See the worst deeds they prompt, shall sink
      for ever?
No, I am hardened
   Ors. Why, what need of. this?
Who feared the pale intrusion of remorse
In a just deed? Altho'our first plan failed
Doubt not but he will soon be laid to rest.
But light the lamp; let us not talk i' the dark.
   Giac. (*Lighting the lamp.*)
And yet once quenched I cannot thus relume
My father's life: do you not think his ghost
Might plead that argument with God?
   Ors. Once gone
You cannot now recall your sister's peace;
Your own extinguished years of youth and hope;
Nor your wife's bitter words; nor all the taunts
Which, from the prosperous, weak misfortune
      takes ;
Nor your dead mother; nor ...
   Giac. O, speak no more!
I am resolved, although this very hand
Must quench the life that animated it.
   Ors. There is no need of that. Listen : you
      know
Olimpio, the castellan of Petrella
In old Colonna's time; him whom your father
Degraded from his post? And Marzio,

That desperate wretch , whom he deprived last
    year
Of a reward of blood, well earned and due?
  Giac. I knew Olimpio ; and they say he
    hated
Old Cenci so, that in his silent rage
His lips grew white only to see him pass.
Of Marzio I know nothing.
  Ors. Marzio's hate
Matches Olimpio's. I have sent these men,
But in your name, and as at your request,
To talk with Beatrice and Lucretia.
  Giac. Only to talk?
  Ors. The moments which even now
Pass onward to morrow's midnight hour
May memorize their flight with death: ere then
They must have talked, and may perhaps have
    done,
And made an end....
  Giac. Listen! What sound is that ?
  Ors. The housedog moans, and the beams
    crack: nought else.
  Giac. It is my wife complaining in her sleep:
I doubt not she is saying bitter things
Of me ; and all my children round her dreaming
That I deny them sustenance.
  Ors. Whilst he
Who truly took it from them, and who fills
Their hungry rest with bitterness, now sleeps
Lapped in bad pleasures, and triumphantly

Mocks thee in visions of successful hate
Too like the truth of day.
   Giac. If e'er he wakes
Again, I will not trust to hireling hands ...
   Ors· Why, that were well. I must be gone ;
       good night!
When next we meet ...
   Giac. May all be done – and all
Forgotten – Oh, that I had never been!
                 (*exeunt.*)

END OF THE THIRD ACT.

A C T IV.

SCENE I.

An apartment in the Castle of Petrella
Enter CENCI.

Cen. She comes not; yet I left her even now
Vanquished and faint. She knows the penalty
Of her delay: yet what if threats are vain?
Am I now not within Petrella's moat?
Or fear I still the eyes and ears of Rome?
Might I not drag her by the golden hair?
Stamp on her? Keep her sleepless till her brain
Be overworn? Tame her with chains and famine?
Less would suffice. Yet so to leave undone
What I most seek! No, 'tis her stubborn will
Which by its own consent shall stoop as low
As that which drags it down.
        Enter LUCRETIA.
                Thou loathed wretch!
Hide thee from my abhorrence; Fly, begone!
Yet stay! Bid Beatrice come hither.
    Lucr. Oh,
Husband! I pray for thine own wretched sake
Heed what thou dost. A man who walks like thee
Thro' crimes, and thro' the danger of his crimes,
Each hour may stumble o'er a sudden grave.
And thou art old; thy hairs are hoary gray;

As thou wouldst save thyself from death and hell,
Pity thy daughter; give her to some friend
In marriage: so that she may tempt thee not
To hatred, or worse thoughts, if worse there be.

   Cen. What! like her sister who has found a home
To mock my hate from with prosperity?
Strange ruin shall destroy both her and thee
And all that yet remain. My death may be
Rapid, her destiny outspeeds it. Go,
Bid her come hither, and before my mood
Be changed, lest I should drag her by the hair

   Lucr. She sent me to thee, husband. At thy
      presence
She fell, as thou dost know, into a trance;
And in that trance she heard a voice which said,
» Cenci must die! Let him confess himself!
» Even now the accusing Angel waits to hear
» If God, to punish his enormous crimes,
» Harden his dying heart!

   Cen. Why - such things are ...
No doubt divine revealings may be made.
'Tis plain I have been favoured from above,
For when I cursed my sons they died. – Aye ... so...
As to the right or wrong thats talk ... repentance...
Repentance is an easy moment's work
And more depends on God than me. Well ... well ...
I must give up the greater point, which was
To poison and corrupt her soul.

     (*A pause; Lucretia approaches anxiously, and
      then shrinks back as he speaks.*)

One, two;
Aye ... Rocco and Cristofano my curse
Strangled: and Giacomo, I think, will find
Life a worse Hell than that beyond the grave :
Beatrice shall, if there be skill in hate
Die in despair, blaspheming: to Bernardo,
He is so innocent, I will bequeath
The memory of these deeds, and make his youth
The sepulchre of hope, where evil thoughts
Shall grow like weeds on a neglected tomb.
When all is done, out in the wide Campagna,
I will pile up my silver and my gold;
My costly robes, paintings and tapestries;
My parchments and all records of my wealth,
And make a bonfire in my joy, and leave
Of my possessions nothing but my name;
Which shall be an inheritance to strip
Its wearer bare as infamy. That done,
My soul, which is a scourge, will I resign
Into the hands of him who wielded it;
Be it for its own punishment or theirs,
He will not ask it of me till the lash
Be broken in its last and deepest wound;
Untill its hate be all inflicted. Yet,
Lest death outspeed my purpose, let me make
Short work and sure ...   (*going*)
    Lucr. (*Stops him*) Oh, stay! It was a feint:
She had no vision, and she heard no voice.
I said it but to awe thee.
    Cen. That is well.

Vile palterer with the sacred truth of God,
Be thy soul choked with that blaspheming lie!
For Beatrice worse terrors are in store
To bend her to my will.

 Lucr. Oh! to what will?
What cruel sufferings more than she has known
Canst thou inflict?

 Cen. Andrea! Go call my daughter,
And if she comes not tell her that I come.
What sufferings? I will drag her, step by step,
Thro' infamies unheard of among men:
She shall stand shelterless in the broad noon
Of public scorn, for acts blazoned abroad,
One among which shall be ... What? Canst thou
    guess?
She shall become, (for what she most abhors
Shall have a fascination to entrap
Her loathing will), to her own conscious self
All she appears to others; and when dead,
As she shall die unshrived and unforgiven,
A rebel to her father and her God,
Her corpse shall be abandoned to the hounds;
Her name shall be the terror of the earth;
Her spirit shall approach the throne of God
Plague spotted with my curses. I will make
Body and soul a monstrous lump of ruin.

    Enter ANDREA.

 Andr. The lady Beatrice ...

 Cen. Speak, pale slave! What
Said she?

Andr. My Lord, 'twas what she looked; she
     said :
Go tell my father that I see the gulph
Of Hell between us two, which he may pass,
I will not.
                  (*Exit* ANDREA.)

  Cen. Go thou quick, Lucretia,
Tell her to come; yet let her understand
Her coming is consent: and say, moreover,
That if she come not I will curse her.
                (*Exit* LUCRETIA.)
               Ha !
With what but with a father's curse doth God
Panic-strike armed victory, and make pale
Cities in their prosperity? The world's Father
Must grant a parent's prayer against his child
Be he who asks even what men call me.
Will not the deaths of her rebellious brothers
Awe her before I speak? For I on them
Did imprecate quick ruin, and it came.
        Enter LUCRETIA
Well; what? Speak, wretch !
  Lucr. She said, I cannot come ;
Go tell my father that I see a torrent
Of his own blood raging between us.
  Cen. (*Kneeling*) God !
Hear me! If this most specious mass of flesh,
Which thou hast made my daughter; this my blood,
This particle of my divided being ;
Or rather, this my bane and my disease ,

Whose sight infects and poisons me; this devil
Which sprung from me as from a hell, was meant
To aught good use; if her bright loveliness
Was kindled to illumine this dark world;
If nursed by thy selectest dew of love
Such virtues blossom in her as should make
The peace of life, I pray thee for my sake,
As thou the common God and Father art
Of her, and me, and all; reverse that doom!
Earth, in the name of God, let her food be
Poison, untill she be encrusted round
With leprous stains! Heaven, rain upon her head
The blistering drops of the Maremma's dew,
Till she be speckled like a toad; parch up
Those love-enkindled lips, warp those fine limbs
To loathed lameness! All beholding sun,
Strike in thine envy those life darting eyes
With thine own blinding beams!
    Lucr. Peace! Peace!
For thine own sake unsay those dreadful words.
When high God grants he punishes such prayers.
    Cen. (*Leaping up, and throwing his right hand*
        towards Heaven)
He does his will, I mine! This in addition,
That if she have a child...
    Lucr. Horrible thought!
    Cen. That if she ever have a child; and thou,
Quick Nature! I adjure thee by thy God,
That thou be fruitful in her, and encrease
And multiply, fulfilling his command,

And my deep imprecation! May it be
A hideous likeness of herself, that as
From a distorting mirror, she may see
Her image mixed with what she most abhors,
Smiling upon her from her nursing breast.
And that the child may from its infancy
Grow, day by day, more wicked and deformed,
Turning her mother's love to misery:
And that both she and it may live until
It shall repay her care and pain with hate,
Or what may else be more unnatural.
So he may hunt her thro' the clamorous scoffs
Of the loud world to a dishonoured grave.
Shall I revoke this curse? Go, bid her come,
Before my words are chronicled in heaven.

                      (*Exit* LUCRETIA)

I do not feel as if I were a man,
But like a fiend appointed to chastise
The offences of some unremembered world.
My blood is running up and down my veins;
A fearful pleasure makes it prick and tingle:
I feel a giddy sickness of strange awe;
My heart is beating with an expectation
Of horrid joy.

            Enter LUCRETIA
            What? Speak!

   Lucr. She bids thee curse;
And if thy curses, as they cannot do,
Could kill her soul ...

   Cen. She would not come. 'Tis well,

I can do both : first take what I demand ,
And then extort concession. To thy chamber !
Fly ere I spurn thee : and beware this night
That thou cross not my footsteps. It were safer
To come between the tiger and his prey.

(*Exit* LUCRETIA)

It must be late; mine eyes grow weary dim
With unaccustomed heaviness of sleep.
Conscience! Oh, thou most insolent of lies!
They say that sleep, that healing dew of heaven,
Steeps not in balm the foldings of the brain
Which thinks thee an impostor. I will go
First to belie thee with an hour of rest,
Which will be deep and calm, I feel: and then...
O, multitudinous Hell, the fiends will shake
Thine arches with the laughter of their joy!
There shall be lamentation heard in Heaven
As o'er an angel fallen; and upon Earth
All good shall droop and sicken, and ill things
Shall with a spirit of unnatural life
Stir and be quickened ... even as I am now.

(*Exit*)

SCENE II.

Before the Castle of Petrella
Enter BEATRICE *and* LUCRETIA *above*
on the ramparts.

Beatr. They come not yet.
Lucr. 'Tis scarce midnight.

Beatr. How slow
Behind the course of thought, even sick with speed.
Lags leaden-footed time!
    Lucr. The minutes pass...
If he should wake before the deed is done?
    Beatr. O, Mother! He must never wake again.
What thou hast said persuades me that our act
Will but dislodge a spirit of deep hell
Out of a human form.
    Lucr. 'Tis true he spoke
Of death and judgement with strange confidence
For one so wicked; as a man believing
In God, yet recking not of good or ill.
And yet to die without confession!...
    Beatr. Oh!
Believe that heaven is merciful and just,
And will not add our dread necessity
To the amount of his offences.
          Enter OLIMPIO *and* MARZIO, *below.*
    Lucr. See,
They come.
    Beatr. All mortal things must hasten thus
To their dark end. Let us go down.
        Exeunt LUCR. *and* BEATR. *from above.*
    Olim. How feel you to this work?
    Mar. As one who thinks
A thousand crowns excellent market price
For an old murderer's life. Your cheeks are pale.
    Olim. It is the white reflexion of your own,
Which you call pale.

Mar. Is that their natural hue?

Olim. Or 'tis my hate and the deferred desire
To wreak it, which extinguishes their blood.

Mar. You are inclined then to this business?

Olim. Aye.
If one should bribe me with a thousand crowns
To kill a serpent which had stung my child,
I could not be more willing.

      Enter BEATRICE *and* LUCRETIA, *below.*
Noble ladies!

Beatr. Are ye resolved?

Olim. Is he asleep?

Mar. Is all
Quiet?

Lucr. I mixed an opiate with his drink:
He sleeps so soundly...

Beatr. That his death will be
But as a change of sin-chastising dreams,
A dark continuance of the Hell within him,
Which God extinguish! But ye are resolved?
Ye know it is a high and holy deed?

Olim. We are resolved.

Mar. As to the how this act
Be warranted, it rests with you.

Beatr. Well, follow!

Olim. Hush! Hark! What noise is that?

Mar. Ha! some one comes!

Beatr. Ye conscience-stricken cravens, rock to
    rest
Your baby hearts. It is the iron gate,

Which ye left open, swinging to the wind,
That enters whistling as in scorn. Come, follow!
And be your steps like mine, light, quick and boid.
                                        (*exeunt.*)

SCENE III.

An apartment in the Castle.
Enter BEATRICE *and* LUCRETIA.

Lucr. They are about it now.
Beatr. Nay, it is done.
Lucr. I have not heard him groan.
Beatr. He will not groan.
Lucr. What sound is that?
Beatr. List! 'tis the tread of feet
About his bed.
Lucr. My God!
If he be now a cold stiff corpse...
Beatr. O, fear not
What may be done, but what is left undone:
The act seals all.
                    Enter OLIMPIO *and* MARZIO.
                    Is it accomplished?
Mar. What?
Olim. Did you not call?
Beatr. When?
Olim. Now.
Beatr. I ask if all is over?
Olim. We dare not kill an old and sleeping man;

His thin grey hair, his stern and reverent brow,
His veined hands crossed on his heaving breast,
And the calm innocent sleep in which he lay,
Quelled me. Indeed, indeed, I cannot do it.

Mar. But I was bolder; for I chid Olimpio,
And bade him bear his wrongs to his own grave
And leave me the reward. And now my knife
Touched the loose wrinkled throat, when the old man
Stirred in his sleep, and said, « God! hear, O, hear,
» A father's curse! What art thou not our father? »
And then he laughed. I knew it was the ghost
Of my dead father speaking through his lips,
And could not kill him.

Beatr. Miserable slaves!
Where, if ye dare not kill a sleeping man,
Found ye the boldness to return to me
With such a deed undone? Base palterers!
Cowards and traitors! Why, the very conscience
Which ye would sell for gold and for revenge
Is an equivocation: it sleeps over
A thousand daily acts disgracing men;
And when a deed where mercy insults heaven...
Why do I talk?

(*Snatching a dagger from one of them
and raising it.*)

Hadst thou a tongue to say,
She murdered her own father, I must do it!
But never dream ye shall outlive him long!

Olim. Stop, for God's sake!

Mar. I will go back and kill him.

Olim. Give me the weapon, we must do thy will.
Beatr. Take it! Depart! Return!

(*Exeunt Olim. and Mar.*)

How pale thou art!
We do but that which 'twere a deadly crime
To leave undone.

Lucr. Would it were done!

Beatr. Even whilst
That doubt is passing through your mind, the world
Is conscious of a change. Darkness and hell
Have swallowed up the vapour they sent forth
To blacken the sweet light of life. My breath
Comes, methinks, lighter and the gellyed blood
Runs freely thro' my veins. Hark!

Enter OLIMPIO *and* MARZIO

He is...

Olim. Dead!

Mar. We strangled him that there might be
no blood;
And then we threw his heavy corpse i' the garden
Under the balcony; 'twill seem it fell.

Beatr. (*giving them a bag of coin*)
Here take this gold, and hasten to your homes.
And, Marzio, because thou wast only awed
By that which made me tremble, wear thou this!

(*Clothes him in a rich mantle*)

It was the mantle which my grandfather
Wore in his high prosperity, and men
Envied his state: so may they envy thine.

Thou wert a weapon in the hand of God
To a just use. Live long and thrive! And, mark,
If thou hast crimes, repent: this deed is none.

    (*A horn is sounded*)

   Lucr. Hark, 'tis the castle horn; my God! it sounds
Like the last trump.

   Beatr. Some tedious guest is coming.

   Lucr. The drawbridge is let down; there is a
      tramp
Of horses in the court; fly, hide yourselves!

      (*Exeunt* OLIM. *and* MAR.)

   Beatr. Let us retire to counterfeit deep rest;
I scarcely need to conterfeit it now:
The spirit which doth reign within these limbs
Seems strangely undisturbed. I could even sleep
Fearless and calm: all ill is surely past.

         (*exeunt*)

SCENE IV.

Another apartment in the Castle.
Enter on one side the Legate SAVELLA
introduced by a servant, and on the other
LUCRETIA *and* BERNARDO.

   Sav. Lady, my duty to his Holiness
Be my excuse that thus unseasonably
I break upon your rest. I must speak with
Count Cenci; doth he sleep?

   Lucr. (*In a hurried and confused manner*)
     I think he sleeps;

Yet wake him not, I pray, spare me awhile,
He is a wicked and wrathful man;
Should he be roused out of his sleep to night,
Which is, I know, a hell of angry dreams,
It were not well; indeed it were not well.
Wait till day break. ...
       (*aside*) O, I am deadly sick!
 Sav. I grieve thus to distress you, but the Count
Must answer charges of the gravest import,
And suddenly; such my commission is.
 Lucr. (*With increased agitation*)
I dare not rouse him: I know none who dare ...
'Twere perilous;... you might as safely waken
A serpent; or a corpse in which some fiend
Were laid to sleep.
 Sav. Lady, my moments here
Are counted. I must rouse him from his sleep,
Since none else dare.
 Lucr. (*aside*) O, terror! O, despair!
(*to Bernardo*) Bernardo, conduct you the Lord Legate to
Your father's chamber.
      (*exeunt* SAV. *and* BERN.)
    enter BEATRICE
 Beatr. 'Tis a messenger
Come to arrest the culprit who now stands
Before the throne of unappealable God.
Both Earth and Heaven, consenting arbiters,
Acquit our deed.

Lucr. Oh, agony of fear!
Would that he yet might live! Even now I heard
The legate's followers whisper as they passed
They had a warrant for his instant death.
All was prepared by unforbidden means
Which we must pay so dearly, having done.
Even now they search the tower, and find the body;
Now they suspect the truth; now they consult
Before they come to tax us with the fact;
O, horrible, 'tis all discovered!
  Beatr. Mother,
What is done wisely, is done well. Be bold
As thou art just. 'Tis like a truant child
To fear that others know what thou hast done,
Even from thine own strong consciousness, and thus
Write on unsteady eyes and altered cheeks
All thou wouldst hide. Be faithful to thyself,
And fear no other witness but thy fear.
For if, as cannot be, some circumstance
Should rise in accusation, we can blind
Suspicion with such cheap astonishment,
Or overbear it with such guiltless pride,
As murderers cannot feign. The deed is done,
And what may follow now regards not me.
I am as universal as the light;
Free as the earth-surrounding air; as firm
As the world's centre. Consequence, to me,
Is as the wind which strikes the solid rock
But shakes it not.
     (*A cry within and tumult*)

Murder! Murder! Murder!

Enter BERNARDO *and* SAVELLA

Sav. (*to his followers*)

Go, search the castle round; sound the alarm;
Look to the gates that none escape!

Beatr. What now?

Ber. I know not what to say ... my father's dead.

Beatr. How; dead! he only sleeps; you mistake,
    brother.

His sleep is very calm, very like death;
'Tis wonderful how well a tyrant sleeps.
He is not dead?

Ber. Dead; murdered.

Lucr. (*With extreme agitation*) Oh, no, no,
He is not murdered though he may be dead;
I have alone the keys of those apartments.

Sav. Ha! Is it so?

Beatr. My Lord, I pray excuse us;
We will retire; my mother is not well:
She seems quite overcome with this strange horror.

         (*exeunt* LUCR. *and* BEATR.)

Sav. Can you suspect who may have murdered
    him?

Ber. I know not what to think.

Sav. Can you name any
Who had an interest in his death?

Ber. Alas!
I can name none who had not, and those most
Who most lament that such a deed is done;
My mother, and my sister, and myself.

10

Sav. 'Tis strange! There were clear marks of
    violence.
I found the old man's body in the moonlight
Hanging beneath the window of his chamber
Among the branches of a pine: he could not
Have fallen there, for all his limbs lay heaped
And effortless; 'tis true there was no blood...
Favour me, Sir; it much imports your house
That all should be made clear; to tell the ladies
That I request their presence.

                  (*exit* BER.)

    Enter Guards bringing in MARZIO
Guard. We have one.
Officer. My Lord, we found this ruffian• and
    another
Lurking among the rocks; there is no doubt
But that they are the murderers of Count Cenci:
Each had a bag of coin; this fellow wore
A gold-inwoven robe, which shining bright
Under the dark rocks to the glimmering moon
Betrayed them to our notice: the other fell
Desperately fighting.
    Sav. What does he confess?
    Officer. He keeps firm silence; but these lines
    found on him
May speak.
    Sav. Their language is at least sincere.

                  (*reads*)

      To THE LADY BEATRICE.
» That the atonement of what my nature

» Sickens to conjecture may soon arrive,
» I send thee, at thy brother's desire, those
» Who will speak and do more than I dare
» Write ... Thy devoted servant,

ORSINO.

Enter LUCRETIA, BEATRICE *and* BERNARDO.

Knowest thou this writing, Lady?

Beatr. No.

Sav. Nor thou?

Lucr. (*Her conduct throughout the scene is marked by extreme agitation.*)

Where was it found? What is it? It should be
Orsino's hand! It speaks of that strange horror
Which never yet found utterance, but which made
Between that hapless child and her dead father
A gulph of obscure hatred

Sav. Is it so?

Is it true, Lady, that thy father did
Such outrages as to awaken in thee
Unfilial hate?

Beatr. Not hate, 'twas more than hate:
This is most true, yet wherefore question me?

Sav. There is a deed demanding question done;
Thou hast a secret which will answer not.

Beatr. What sayest? My Lord, your words are
bold and rash.

Sav. I do arrest all present in the name
Of the Pope's Holiness. You must to Rome.

Lucr. O, not to Rome! Indeed we are not
guilty

Beatr. Guilty! Who dares talk of guilt? My
  Lord,
I am more innocent of parricide
Than is a child born fatherless ... Dear Mother,
Your gentleness and patience are no shield
For this keen judging world, this two edged lie,
Which seems, but is not. What! will human laws,
Rather will ye who are their ministers·,
Bar all access to retribution first,
And then, when heaven doth interpose to do
What ye neglect, arming familiar things
To the redress of an unwonted crime,
Make ye the victims who demanded it
Culprits? 'Tis ye are culprits! That poor wretch
Who stands so pale, and trembling, and amazed,
If it be true he murdered Cenci, was
A sword in the right hand of justest God,
Wherefore should I have wielded it? Unless
The crimes which mortal tongue dare never name
God therefore scruples to avenge.
  Sav. You own
That you desired his death?
  Beatr. It would have been
A crime no less than his, if for one moment
That fierce desire had faded in my heart.
'Tis true I did believe, and hope, and pray,
Aye, I even knew... for God is wise and just,
That some strange sudden death hung over him.
'Tis true that this did happen, and most true
There was no other rest for me on earth,

No other hope in Heaven ... now what of this?
 Sav. Strange thoughts beget strange deeds; and
  here are both:
I judge thee not.
 Beatr. And yet, if you arrest me,
You are the judge and executioner
Of that which is the life of life: the breath
Of accusation kills an innocent name,
And leaves for lame acquittal the poor life
Which is a mask without it. 'Tis most false
That I am guilty of foul parricide;
Although I must rejoice, for justest cause,
That other hands have sent my father's soul
To ask the mercy he denied to me.
Now leave us free: stain not a noble house
With vague surmises of rejected crime;
Add to our sufferings and your own neglect
No heavier sum: let them have been enough:
Leave us the wreck we have.
 Sav. I dare not, Lady.
I pray that you prepare yourselves for Rome:
There the Pope's further pleasure will be known.
 Lucr. O, not to Rome! O, take us not to Rome!
 Beatr. Why not to Rome, dear mother? There
  as here
Our innocence is as an armed heel
To trample accusation. God is there
As here, and with his shadow ever clothes
The innocent, the injured and the weak;
And such are we. Cheer up, dear Lady, lean

On me; collect your wandering thoughts. My Lord,
As soon as you have taken some refreshment,
And had all such examinations made
Upon the spot, as may be necessary
To the full understanding of this matter,
We shall be ready. Mother; will you come?
 Lucr. Ha ! they will bind us to the rack, and
   wrest
Self-accusation from our agony!
Will Giacomo be there? Orsino? Marzio?
All present; all confronted; all demanding
Each from the others countenance the thing
Which is in every heart! O, misery!
     (*She faints, and is borne out.*)
 Sav. She faints: an ill appearance this.
 Beatr. My Lord,
She knows not yet the uses of the world.
She fears that power is as a beast which grasps
And loosens not: a snake whose look transmutes
All things to guilt which is its nutriment.
She cannot know how well the supine slaves
Of blind authority read the truth of things
When written on a brow of guilelessness:
She sees not yet triumphant Innocence
Stand at the judgement-seat of mortal man,
A judge and an accuser of the wrong
Which drags it there. Prepare yourself, My Lord;
Our suite will join yours in the court below.
       (*Exeunt*)

END OF THE FOURTH ACT.

A C T V.

SCENE I.

An apartment in ORSINO'S *Palace.*
Enter ORSINO *and* GIACOMO.

Giac. Do evil deeds thus quickly come to end?
O, that the vain remorse which must chastise
Crimes done, had but as loud a voice to warn
As its keen sting is mortal to avenge!
O, that the hour when present had cast off
The mantle of its mystery, and shewn
The ghastly form with which it now returns
When its scared game is roused, cheering the
        hounds
Of conscience to their prey! Alas! Alas!
It was a wicked thought, a piteous deed,
To kill an old and hoary-headed father.
  Ors. It has turned out unluckily, in truth.
  Giac. To violate the sacred doors of sleep;
To cheat kind nature of the placid death
Which she prepares for overwearied age;
To drag from Heaven an unrepentant soul
Which might have quenched in reconciling prayers
A life of burning crimes ...
  Ors. You cannot say
I urged you to the deed.
  Giac. O, had I never

Found in thy smooth and ready countenance
The mirror of my darkest thoughts; hadst thou
Never with hints and questions made me look
Upon the monster of my thought, until
It grew familiar to desire ...

   Ors. 'Tis thus
Men cast the blame of their unprosperous acts
Upon the abettors of their own resolve ;
Or any thing but their weak, guilty selves.
And yet, confess the truth, it is the peril
In which you stand that gives you this pale
        sickness
Of penitence ; Confess 'tis fear disguised
From its own shame that takes the mantle now
Of thin remorse. What if we yet were safe ?

   Giac. How can that be ? Already Beatrice,
Lucretia and the murderer are in prison.
I doubt not officers are, whilst we speak,
Sent to arrest us.

   Ors. I have all prepared
For instant flight. We can escape even now,
So we take fleet occasion by the hair.

   Giac. Rather expire in tortures, as I may.
What ! will you cast by self-accusing flight
Assured conviction upon Beatrice ?
She, who alone in this unnatural work,
Stands like God's angel ministered upon
By fiends ; avenging such a nameless wrong
As turns black parricide to piety;
Whilst we for basest ends ... I fear, Orsino,

While I consider all your words and looks,
Comparing them with your proposal now,
That you must be a villain. For what end
Could you engage in such a perilous crime,
Training me on with hints, and signs, and smiles,
Even to this gulph? Thou art no liar? No,
Thou art a lie! Traitor and murderer!
Coward and slave! But, no, defend thyself;

(drawing.)

Let the sword speak what the indignant tongue
Disdains to brand thee with.

   Ors. Put up your weapon.
Is it the desperation of your fear
Makes you thus rash and sudden with a friend,
Now ruined for your sake? If honest anger
Have moved you, know, that what I just proposed
Was but to try you. As for me, I think,
Thankless affection led me to this point,
From which, if my firm temper could repent,
I cannot now recede. Even whilst we speak
The ministers of justice wait below:
They grant me these brief moments. Now if you
Have any word of melancholy comfort
To speak to your pale wife, 'twere best to pass
Out at the postern, and avoid them so.

   Giac. O, generous friend! How canst thou
       pardon me?
Would that my life could purchase thine!

   Ors. That wish
Now comes a day too late. Haste; fare thee well!

11

Hear'st thou not steps along the corridor?

(*Exit Giacomo*)

I'm sorry for it; but the guards are waiting
At his own gate, and such was my contrivance
That I might rid me both of him and them.
I thought to act a solemn comedy
Upon the painted scene of this new world,
And to attain my own peculiar ends
By some such plot of mingled good and ill
As others weave; but there arose a Power
Which graspt and snapped the threads of my device
And turned it to a net of ruin... Ha!

(*a shout is heard*)

Is that my name I hear proclaimed abroad?
But I will pass, wrapt in a vile disguise;
Rags on my back, and a false innocence
Upon my face, thro' the misdeeming crowd
Which judges by what seems. 'Tis easy then
For a new name and for a country new,
And a new life, fashioned on old desires,
To change the honours of abandoned Rome.
And these must be the masks of that within,
Which must remain unaltered... Oh, I fear
That what is past will never let me rest!
Why, when none else is conscious, but myself,
Of my misdeeds, should my own heart's contempt
Trouble me? Have I not the power to fly
My own reproaches? Shall I be the slave
Of... what? A word? which those of this false
        world

Employ against each other, not themselves;
As men wear daggers not for self offence.
But if I am mistaken, where shall I
Find the disguise to hide me from myself,
As now I skulk from every other eye?

(Exit.)

SCENE II.

A Hall of Justice.
CAMILLO, *Judges etc. are discovered seated;*
MARZIO *is led in.*

1. *Judge.* Accused, do you persist in your denial?
I ask you, are you innocent, or guilty?
I demand who were the participators
In your offence? Speak truth and the whole truth.
  Mar. My God! I did not kill him; I know
    nothing;
Olimpio sold the robe to me from which
You would infer my guilt.
  2. *Judge* Away with him!
  1. *Judge* Dare you, with lips yet white from
    the rack's kiss
Speak false? Is it so soft a questioner,
That you would bandy lover's talk with it
Till it wind out your life and soul? Away!
  Mar. Spare me! O, spare! I will confess.
  1. *Judge* Then speak.
  Mar. I strangled him in his sleep.

1. *Judge* Who urged you to it?

Mar. His own son Giacomo, and the young
prelate

Orsino sent me to Petrella; there

The ladies Beatrice and Lucretia

Tempted me with a thousand crowns, and I

And my companion forthwith murdered him.

Now let me die.

    1. *Judge* This sounds as bad as truth. Guards,
there,

Lead forth the prisoners!

  Enter LUCRETIA, BEATRICE *and* GIACOMO, *guarded.*

        Look upon this man;

When did you see him last?

  Beatr. We never saw him.

  Mar. You know me too well, Lady Beatrice.

  Beatr. I know thee! How? where? when?

  Mar. You know 'twas I

Whom you did urge with menaces and bribes

To kill your father. When the thing was done

You clothed me in a robe of woven gold

And bade me thrive: how I have thriven, you see.

You, my Lord Giacomo, Lady Lucretia,

You know that what I speak is true.

    (BEATRICE *advances towards him; he covers*
        his face, and shrinks back.)

      O, dart

The terrible resentment of those eyes

On the dead earth! Turn them away from me!

They wound: 'twas torture forced the truth. My
Lords,

Having said this let me be led to death.
   Beatr. Poor wretch, I pity thee: yet stay awhile.
   Cam. Guards, lead him not away.
   Beatr. Cardinal Camillo,
You have a good repute for gentleness
And wisdom: can it be that you sit here
To countenance a wicked farce like this?
When some obscure, and trembling slave is dragged
From sufferings which might shake the sternest
       heart
And bade to answer, not as he believes,
But as those may suspect or do desire
Whose questions thence suggest their own reply:
And that in peril of such hideous torments
As merciful God spares even the damned. Speak
       now
The thing you surely know, which is that you,
If your fine frame were stretched upon that wheel,
And you were told: Confess that you did poison
Your little nephew; that fair blue-eyed child
Who was the loadstar of your life: and though
All see, since his most swift and piteous death,
That day and night, and heaven and earth, and
       time,
And all the things hoped for or done therein
Are changed to you, through your exceeding grief,
Yet you would say I confess any thing.
And beg from your tormentors, like that slave,
The refuge of dishonourable death.
I pray thee, Cardinal, that thou assert

My innocence.

    Cam. (*Much moved*) What shall we think,
       my lords ?

Shame on these tears! I thought the heart was
    frozen

Which is their fountain. I would pledge my soul

That she is guiltless.

    Judge. Yet she must be tortured.

    Cam I would as soon have tortured mine own
       nephew :

(If he now lived he would be just her age;

His hair, too, was her colour, and his eyes

Like her's in shape, but blue and not so deep)

As that most perfect image of God's love

That ever came sorrowing upon the earth.

She is as pure as speechless infancy!

    Judge. Well, be her purity on your head, my Lord,

If you forbid the rack. His Holiness

Enjoined us to pursue this monstrous crime

By the severest forms of law; nay even

To stretch a point against the criminals.

The prisoners stand accused of parricide

Upon such evidence as justifies

Torture.

    Beatr. What evidence ? This man's ?

    Judge. Even so.

    Beatr. (*to* MARZIO) Come near. And who art
       thou thus chosen forth

Out of the multitude of living men

To kill the innocent ?

Mar. I am Marzio,
Thy father's vassal.
    Beatr. Fix thine eyes on mine ;
Answer to what I ask.

(turning to the Judges)

               I prithee mark
His countenance: unlike bold calumny
Which sometimes dares not speak the thing it
        looks,
He dares not look the thing he speaks, but bends
His gaze on the blind earth.

(to MARZIO)

              What ! wilt thou say
That I did murder my own father ?
    Mar. Oh !
Spare me ! My brain swims round...I cannot speak...
It was that horrid torture forced the truth.
Take me away ! Let her not look on me !
I am a guilty miserable wretch ;
I have said all I know ; now, let me die !
    Beatr. My Lords, if by my nature I had been
So stern, as to have planned the crime alledged,
Which your suspicions dictate to this slave,
And the rack makes him utter, do you think
I should have left this two edged instrument
Of my misdeed ; this man, this bloody knife
With my own name engraven on the heft,
Lying unsheathed amid' a world of foes,
For my own death ? That with such horrible need
For deepest silence, I should have neglected

So trivial a precaution, as the making
His tomb the keeper of a secret written
On a thief's memory ? What is his poor life ?
What are a thousand lives ? A parricide
Had trampled them like dust; and, see, he lives!

(*turning to* MARZIO)

And thou ...

Mar. Oh, spare me! Speak to me no more!
That stern yet piteous look, those solemn tones,
Wound worse than torture.

(*to the Judges*)
I have told it all;
For pity's sake lead me away to death .

Cam. Guards, lead him nearer the lady Beatrice,
He shrinks from her regard like autumn's leaf
From the keen breath of the serenest north.

Beatr. Oh , thou who tremblest on the giddy
verge
Of life and death, pause ere thou answerest me;
So mayest thou answer God with less dismay:
What evil have we done thee ? I, alas!
Have lived but on this earth a few sad years
And so my lot was ordered, that a father
First turned the moments of awakening life
To drops, each poisoning youth's sweet hope ;
and then
Stabbed with one blow my everlasting soul ;
And my untainted fame ; and even that peace
Which sleeps within the core of the heart's heart;
But the wound was not mortal; so my hate

Became the only worship I could lift
To our great father, who in pity and love,
Armed thee, as thou dost say, to cut him off;
And thus his wrong becomes my accusation;
And art thou the accuser? If thou hopest
Mercy in heaven, shew justice upon earth:
Worse than a bloody hand is a hard heart.
If thou hast done murders, made thy life's path
Over the trampled laws of God and man,
Rush not before thy Judge, and say: » My maker,
» I have done this and more; for there was one
» Who was most pure and innocent on earth;
» And because she endured what never any
» Guilty or innocent endured before:
» Because her wrongs could not be told, not
             thought;
» Because thy hand at length did rescue her;
» I with my words killed her and all her kin.»
Think, I adjure you, what it is to slay
The reverence living in the minds of men
Towards our ancient house, and stainless fame!
Think what it is to strangle infant pity,
Cradled in the belief of guileless looks,
Till it become a crime to suffer. Think
What 'tis to blot with infamy and blood
All that which shews like innocence, and is,
Hear me, great God! I swear, most innocent,
So that the world lose all discrimination
Between the sly, fierce, wild regard of guilt,
And that which now compels thee to reply

To what I ask: Am I, or am I not
A parricide?

Mar. Thou art not!

Judge. What is this?

Mar. I here declare those whom I did accuse
Are innocent. 'Tis I alone am guilty.

Judge. Drag him away to torments; let them be
Subtle and long drawn out, to tear the folds
Of the heart's inmost cell. Unbind him not
Till he confess.

Mar. Torture me as ye will:
A keener pain has wrung a higher truth
From my last breath. She is most innocent!
Bloodhounds, not men, glut yourselves well
      with me;
I will not give you that fine piece of nature
To rend and ruin.

                  (*exit* MARZIO, *guarded*)

Cam. What say ye now, my Lords?

Judge. Let tortures strain the truth till it be
white
As snow thrice sifted by the frozen wind.

Cam. Yet stained with blood.

Judge. (to Beatrice) Know you this paper, Lady?

Beatr. Entrap me not with questions. Who
stands here
As my accuser? Ha! wilt thou be he,
Who art my judge? Accuser, witness, judge,
What, all in one? Here is Orsino's name;
Where is Orsino? Let his eye meet mine.

What means this scrawl? Alas! Ye know not what,
And therefore on the chance that it may be
Some evil, will ye kill us?
                    Enter an officer.
  Officer. Marzio's dead.
  Judge. What did he say?
  Officer Nothing. As soon as we
Had bound him on the wheel, he smiled on us,
As one who baffles a deep adversary;
And holding his breath, died.
  Judge There remains nothing
But to apply the question to those prisoners,
Who yet remain stubborn.
  Cam. I overrule
Further proceedings, and in the behalf
Of these most innocent and noble persons
Will use my interest with the Holy Father.
  Judge Let the Pope's pleasure then be done.
          Meanwhile
Conduct these culprits each to separate cells;
And be the engines ready: for this night
If the Pope's resolution be as grave,
Pious and just as once, I'll wring the truth
Out of those nerves and sinews, groan by groan.
                              (*Exeunt.*)

SCENE III.

The cell of a prison.
BEATRICE *is discovered asleep on a couch;*
enter BERNARDO.

Ber. How gently slumber rests upon her face,
Like the last thoughts of some day sweetly spent
Closing in night and dreams, and so prolonged.
After such torments as she bore last night,
How light and soft her breathing comes. Ay, me!
Methinks that I shall never sleep again.
But I must shake the heavenly dew of rest
From this sweet folded flower, thus ... wake!
    awake!
What, sister, canst thou sleep?
    Beatr. (*awaking*) I was just dreaming
That we were all in Paradise. Thou knowest
This cell seems like a kind of Paradise
After our father's presence.
    Ber. Dear, dear sister,
Would that thy dream were not a dream! O, God!
How shall I tell?
    Beatr. What wouldst thou tell, sweet brother?
    Ber. Look not so calm and happy, or even
    whilst
I stand considering what I have to say
My heart will break.
    Beatr. See now, thou mak'st me weep:
How very friendless thou would'st be, dear child,

If I were dead. Say what thou hast to say.
 Ber. They have confessed ; they could endure
   no more
The tortures ...
 Beatr. Ha ! What was there to confess ?
They must have told some weak and wicked lie
To flatter their tormentors. Have they said
That they were guilty ? O, white innocence,
That thou shouldst wear the mask of guilt to hide
Thine awful and serenest countenance
From those who know thee not !
 Enter JUDGE *with* LUCRETIA *and* GIACOMO, *guarded*
   Ignoble hearts !
For some brief spasms of pain, which are at least
As mortal as the limbs through which they pass,
Are centuries of high splendour laid in dust?
And that eternal honour which should live
Sunlike, above the reek of mortal fame,
Changed to a mockery and a bye-word? What!
Will you give up these bodies to be dragged
At horse's heels, so that our hair should sweep
The footsteps of the vain and senseless crowd,
Who, that they may make our calamity
Their worship and their spectacle, will leave
The churches and the theatres as void
As their own hearts ? Shall the light multitude
Fling, at their choice, curses or faded pity,
Sad funeral flowers to deck a living corpse,
Upon us as we pass to pass away,
And leave ... what memory of our having been?

Infamy, blood, terror, despair? O thou,
Who wert a mother to the parentless
Kill not thy child! Let not her wrongs kill thee!
Brother, lie down with me upon the rack,
And let us each be silent as a corpse;
It soon will be as soft as any grave.
'Tis but the falsehood it can wring from fear
Makes the rack cruel.
 Giac. They will tear the truth
Even from thee at last, those cruel pains:
For pity's sake say thou art guilty now.
 Lucr. O, speak the truth! Let us all quickly die;
And after death, God is our judge, not they;
He will have mercy on us.
 Ber. If indeed
It can be true, say so, dear sister mine;
And then the Pope will surely pardon you,
And all be well.
 Judge. Confess, or I will warp
Your limbs with such keen tortures ...
 Beatr. Tortures! Turn
The rack henceforth into a spinning wheel!
Torture your dog, that he may tell when last
He lapped the blood his master shed... not me!
My pangs are of the mind, and of the heart,
And of the soul; aye, of the inmost soul,
Which weeps within tears as of burning gall
To see, in this ill world where none are true,
My kindred false to their deserted selves.
And with considering all the wretched life

Which I have lived, and its now wretched end,
And the small justice shewn by Heaven and Earth
To me or mine; and what a tyrant thou art,
And what slaves these; and what a world we make,
The oppressor and the oppressed.... such pangs
     compel
My answer. What is it thou wouldst with me?
    Judge. Art thou not guilty of thy father's death?
    Beatr. Or wilt thou rather tax high judging God
That he permitted such an act as that
Which I have suffered, and which he beheld;
Made it unutterable, and took from it
All refuge, all revenge, all consequence,
But that which thou hast called my father's death?
Which is or is not what men call a crime,
Which either I have done, or have not done;
Say what ye will. I shall deny no more.
If ye desire it thus, thus let it be,
And so an end of all. Now do your will;
No other pains shall force another word.
    Judge She is convicted, but has not confessed.
Be it enough. Until their final sentence
Let none have converse with them. You, young
    Lord ,
Linger not here !
    Beatr. O , tear him not away !
    Judge Guards do your duty.
    Ber. (*Embracing* BEATRICE) Oh! would ye divide
Body from soul?
    Officer. That is the headsman's business.

(*Exeunt all but* LUCR. BEATR. *and* GIAC.)

Giac. Have I confessed? Is it all over now?
No hope! No refuge! O, weak, wicked tongue
Which hast destroyed me would that thou hadst been
Cut out and thrown to dogs first? To have killed
My father first, and then betrayed my sister;
Aye, thee! the one thing innocent and pure
In this black guilty world, to that which I
So well deserve! My wife! my little ones!
Destitute, helpless and I... Father! God!
Canst thou forgive even the unforgiving,
When their full hearts break thus, thus!..

                 (*Covers his face and weeps*)

    Lucr. O, my child!
To what a dreadful end are we all come!
Why did I yield? Why did I not sustain
Those torments? Oh, that I were all dissolved
Into these fast and unavailing tears,
Which flow and feel not!

        Beatr. What 'twas weak to do,
'Tis weaker to lament, once being done;
Take cheer! The God who knew my wrong, and made
           made
Our speedy act the angel of his wrath,
Seems, and but seems to have abandoned us.
Let us not think that we shall die for this.
Brother, sit near me; give me your firm hand,
You had a manly heart. Bear up! Bear up!
O, dearest Lady, put your gentle head
Upon my lap, and try to sleep awhile:

Your eyes look pale, hollow and overworn,
With heaviness of watching and slow grief.
Come, I will sing you some low, sleepy tune,
Not cheerful, nor yet sad; some dull old thing ,
Some outworn and unused monotony ,
Such as our country gossips sing and spin,
Till they almost forget they live: lie down!
So, that will do. Have I forgot the words?
Faith! They are sadder than I thought they were.

SONG

False friend , wilt thou smile or weep
When my life is laid asleep?
Little cares for a smile or a tear,
The clay-cold corpse upon the bier!
  Farewell! Heighho !
  What is this whispers low ?
There is a snake in thy smile , my dear;
And bitter poison within thy tear.

Sweet sleep, were death like to thee,
Or if thou couldst mortal be ,
I would close these eyes of pain;
When to wake? Never again.
  O, World! Farewell!
  Listen to the passing bell!
It says, thou and I must part,
With a light and a heavy heart.

    (*The scene closes.*)
    13

SCENE IV.

A Hall of the Prison.

Enter CAMILLO *and* BERNARDO.

Cam. The Pope is stern; not to be moved
　　or bent.
He looked as calm and keen as is the engine
Which tortures and which kills, exempt itself
From aught that it inflicts; a marble form,
A rite, a law, a custom: not a man.
He frowned, as if to frown had been the trick
Of his machinery, on the advocates
Presenting the defences, which he tore
And threw behind, muttering with hoarse, harsh
　　voice:
» Which among ye defended their old father
» Killed in his sleep? » Then to another: » Thou
» Dost this in virtue of thy place; 'tis well. »
He turned to me then, looking deprecation,
And said these three words, coldly: » They
　　must die . »
　　Ber. And yet you left him not?
　　Cam. I urged him still;
Pleading, as I could guess, the devilish wrong
Which prompted your unnatural parent's death.
And he replied. » Paolo Santa Croce
» Murdered his mother yester evening,
» And he is fled. Parricide grows so rife

» That soon, for some just cause   no   doubt, the
     young
» Will strangle us all, dozing in our chairs.
» Authority, and power, and hoary hair
» Are grown crimes capital. You are my nephew,
» You come to ask their pardon; stay a moment;
» Here is their sentence ; never see me more
» Till, to the letter, it be all fulfilled. »

    Ber. O, God, not so ! I did believe indeed
That all you said was but sad preparation
For happy news. O, there are words and looks
To bend the sternest purpose! Once I knew them,
Now I forget them at my dearest need.
What think you if I seek him out, and bathe
His feet and robe with hot and bitter tears?
Importune him with prayers, vexing his brain
With my perpetual cries, until in rage
He strike me with his pastoral cross, and trample
Upon my prostrate head, so that my blood
May stain the senseless dust on which he treads,
And remorse waken mercy? I will do it!
O, wait till I return !   (*rushes out.*)

    Cam. Alas! poor boy !
A wreck-devoted seaman thus might pray
To the deaf sea.

    Enter LUCRETIA , BEATRICE *and* GIACOMO, *guarded.*

    Beatr. I hardly dare to fear
That thou bring'st other news than a just pardon.

    Cam. May God in heaven be less inexorable
To the Pope's prayers, than he has been to mine.

Here is the sentence and the warrant.
   Beatr. (*Wildly*) Oh,
My God! Can it be possible I have
To die so suddenly? So young to go
Under the obscure, cold, rotting, wormy ground!
To be nailed down into a narrow place;
To see no more sweet sunshine; hear no more
Blithe voice of living thing; muse not again
Upon familiar thoughts, sad, yet thus lost
How fearful! to be nothing! Or to be ...
What? O, where am I? Let me not go mad!
Sweet Heaven, forgive weak thoughts! If there
     should be
No God, no Heaven, no Earth in the void world;
The wide, grey, lampless, deep, unpeopled world!
If all things then should be ... my father's spirit
His eye, his voice, his touch surrounding me;
The atmosphere and breath of my dead life!
If sometimes, as a shape more like himself,
Even the form which tortured me on earth,
Masked in grey hairs and wrinkles, he should
     come
And wind me in his hellish arms, and fix
His eyes on mine, and drag me down, down,
     down!
For was he not alone omnipotent
On Earth, and ever present? Even tho'dead,
Does not his spirit live in all that breathe,
And work for me and mine still the same ruin,
Scorn, pain, despair? Who ever yet returned

To teach the laws of death's untrodden realm?
Unjust perhaps as those which drive us now,
O, whither, whither?
   Lucr. Trust in God's sweet love,
The tender promises of Christ: ere night
Think we shall be in Paradise.
   Beatr. 'Tis past!
Whatever comes my heart shall sink no more.
And yet, I know not why, your words strike chill:
How tedious, false and cold seem all things. I
Have met with much injustice in this world;
No difference has been made by God or man,
Or any power moulding my wretched lot,
'Twixt good or evil, as regarded me.
I am cut off from the only world I know,
From light, and life, and love, in youth's sweet
      prime.
You do well telling me to trust in God,
I hope I do trust in him. In whom else
Can any trust? And yet my heart is cold.
   (*During the latter speeches* GIACOMO *has retired
     conversing with* CAMILLO, *who now goes out;*
     GIACOMO *advances*)
   Giac. Know you not, Mother... Sister, know
     you not?
Bernardo even now is gone to implore
The Pope to grant our pardon.
   Lucr. Child, perhaps
It will be granted. We may all then live
To make these woes a tale for distant years:

O, what a thought! It gushes to my heart
Like the warm blood.
  Beatr. Yet both will soon be cold.
O, trample out that thought! Worse than despair,
Worse than the bitterness of death, is hope:
It is the only ill which can find place
Upon the giddy, sharp and narrow hour
Tottering beneath us. Plead with the swift frost
That it should spare the eldest flower of spring:
Plead with awakening Earthquake, o'er whose couch
Even now a city stands, strong, fair and free;
Now stench and blackness yawns, like death. O,
   plead
With famine, or wind-walking Pestilence,
Blind lightning, or the deaf sea, not with man!
Cruel, cold, formal man; righteous in words,
In deeds a Cain. No, Mother, we must die:
Since such is the reward of innocent lives;
Such the alleviation of worst wrongs.
And whilst our murderers live, and hard, cold
   men,
Smiling and slow, walk thro' a world of tears
To death as to life's sleep; 'twere just the grave
Were some strange joy for us. Come, obscure
   Death,
And wind me in thine all-embracing arms!
Like a fond mother hide me in thy bosom,
And rock me to the sleep from which none wake.
Live ye, who live, subject to one another
As we were once, who now...

BERNARDO *rushes in.*

Ber. Oh, horrible!
That tears, that looks, that hope poured forth
        in prayer,
Even till the heart is vacant and despairs,
Should all be vain! The ministers of death
Are waiting round the doors. I thought I saw
Blood on the face of one... what if 'twere fancy?
Soon the heart's blood of all I love on earth
Will sprinkle him, and he will wipe it off
As if 'twere only rain. O, life! O, world!
Cover me! let me be no more! To see
That perfect mirror of pure innocence
Wherein I gazed, and grew happy and good,
Shivered to dust! To see thee, Beatrice,
Who made all lovely thou didst look upon...
Thee, light of life... dead, dark! while I say, sister,
To hear I have no sister; and thou, Mother,
Whose love was a bond to all our loves...
Dead! The sweet bond broken!

                Enter CAMILLO *and Guards.*

        They come! Let me
Kiss those warm lips before their crimson leaves
Are blighted ... white... cold. Say farewell, before
Death chokes that gentle voice! O, let me hear
You speak!

Beatr. Farewell, my tender brother. Think
Of our sad fate with gentleness, as now:
And let mild, pitying thoughts lighten for thee
Thy sorrow's load. Err not in harsh despair,

But tears and patience. One thing more, my child,
For thine own sake be constant to the love
Thou bearest us; and to the faith that I,
Tho' wrapt in a strange cloud of crime and
      shame,
Lived ever holy and unstained. And tho'
Ill tongues shall wound me, and our common
      name
Be as a mark stamped on thine innocent brow
For men to point at as they pass, do thou
Forbear, and never think a thought unkind
Of those, who perhaps love thee in their graves.
So mayest thou die as I do; fear and pain
Being subdued. Farewell! Farewell! Farewell!

   Ber. I cannot say, farewell!

   Cam. O, Lady Beatrice!

   Beatr. Give yourself no unnecessary pain,
My dear Lord Cardinal. Here, Mother, tie
My girdle for me, and bind up this hair
In any simple knot; aye, that does well.
And yours I see is coming down. How often
Have we done this for one another; now
We shall not do it any more. My Lord,
We are quite ready. Well, 'tis very well.

THE END.